THE MASS MEDIA IN CAMPAIGN '84

articles from Public Opinion magazine

edited by Michael J. Robinson and Austin Ranney

American Enterprise Institute for Public Policy Research
Washington, D.C.

Distributed by arrangement with
UPA, Inc.
4720 Boston Way, Lanham, MD 20706
3 Henrietta Street, London, WC2E 8LU England

ISBN 0-8447-3582-5
AEI Studies 426

Library of Congress Catalog Card Number 85-71698

Printed in the United States of America

Contents

Contributors

WILLIAM C. ADAMS
is an associate professor of public administration at
George Washington University.

STEPHEN BATES
is a student at
Harvard University's Law School.

MAURA CLANCEY
is a provost fellow in the Arts and Humanities Division of
the University of Maryland.

EDWIN DIAMOND
is an adjunct professor in the
Department of Political Science at the
Massachusetts Institute of Technology.

LAURILY EPSTEIN
is a polling consultant to NBC News.

BARBARA G. FARAH
is director of news surveys at the *New York Times*.

DAVID GERGEN
is an AEI visiting fellow in communications and a
fellow at Harvard's Institute of Politics.

DAVID MOORE
is an associate professor of political science at the Univerity of
New Hampshire and codirector of the New Hampshire poll.

HOWARD PENNIMAN
is an AEI resident scholar and
codirector of AEI's Political and Social Processes Program.

AUSTIN RANNEY
is a resident scholar at AEI and
codirector of AEI's Political and Social Processes Program.

MICHAEL J. ROBINSON
is a visiting scholar at AEI and
director of the Media Analysis Project at George Washington University

GERALD STROM
is an associate professor of political science at the
University of Illinois at Chicago.

NICK THIMMESCH
is resident journalist at AEI and a syndicated columnist.

Foreword

Suspicion of the media has been a persistent strain in American history. In the early 1800s, for example, James Fenimore Cooper said, "If newspapers are useful in overthrowing tyrants, it is only to establish a tyranny of their own." Today the political arena is perceived by some to be a media marketplace: he or she who "gets good press" gets elected. The losing presidential candidate in 1984, for one, blames his loss on a failure to communicate his message rather than on a failure of the message itself. The media are seen by some to be all-powerful in determining the outcome of elections.

Now comes a new group of studies, recently published in *Public Opinion* magazine and collected here, that challenge many widely held views about the role of the media in the American electoral system. The candidates who get the most negative coverage do not necessarily lose, according to new research on the 1984 campaign. Candidates who spend the most money on media ads, in fact, do not necessarily win—the candidates who spent the most in the 1984 Democratic primary races lost those primaries.

The articles collected here allow for guarded optimism about both the media and their audiences. The people show a healthy skepticism toward the media, it seems, and the media in turn show a healthy respect for that skepticism. Those who would try to slant our votes or our thinking have their work cut out for them.

The range of articles presented here and the credentials of these distinguished authors offer an illustration of the broad scope of AEI research on the media and their role in American politics. *Public Opinion*, the bimonthly magazine published by AEI to explore the implications of opinion trends, originally published these works and frequently reports on significant media issues. The coeditors of this book, Austin Ranney and

Michael J. Robinson, are deeply involved in AEI's work in this area. Ranney, codirector of AEI's Political and Social Processes program, is the author of *Channels of Power: The Impact of Television on American Politics*. Robinson, an AEI visiting scholar, directs the Media Analysis Project at AEI and George Washington University. The book also includes contributions from Howard Penniman, codirector of AEI's Political and Social Processes program; David Gergen, AEI visiting fellow and former director of the White House Communications Office; and Nick Thimmesch, AEI's resident journalist, who has conducted numerous seminars as part of AEI's Communications in a Free Society project. The proceedings from one such seminar, *Is There a Liberal Media Elite?*, with the publisher Rupert Murdoch and *Washington Post* editor Ben Bradlee, will soon be published by AEI.

The importance of American media has grown dramatically in recent years, but we will not know what this means for our society until much more research is done. Scholars are just beginning to focus close attention on this trend, and the American Enterprise Institute is in the forefront of this effort. This collection represents a significant step forward and, at the same time, suggests a broad range of questions for further study. We are committed in this area—as we are in many other vital areas of public policy—to enhance the competition of ideas and advance the base of knowledge on the media's role in the American political system.

William J. Baroody, Jr.
President
American Enterprise Institute

Introduction

In his first press conference after his crushing defeat by Ronald Reagan in the 1984 presidential election, Walter Mondale offered several explanations for why he had lost. First and foremost, he said, was his poor performance on television. These days political success demands "a mastery of television," and "I didn't like television and television didn't like me." He added that, while that was fair enough in his case, he was concerned that American politics is "losing its substance. It is losing the debate on merit. It is losing the depth. Tough problems require discussion, but more and more it is these twenty-second snippets."

Mondale has a lot of company in believing that the mass communications media, especially television, have become the all-powerful forces in American politics and government. Ever since Joe McGinniss published his book *The Selling of the President 1968*, in which he portrayed Richard Nixon's close win in 1968 as purely the creation of a brilliant advertising campaign, more and more politicians, journalists, and, yes, professors have come to believe that not only have the media become the message but the campaign has become the election. We are now often told that a politician who is "not good on television" cannot hope to win a major office. By the same token, a politician like Ronald Reagan, whose professional skills and experience as a movie actor and television host have made him "the great communicator," can overcome *any* handicap or mistake by using the media to become "Teflon man," the leader to whom nothing bad—no rash statement, no ignorance of facts, no policy failure—ever sticks.

Anything thought to be so critical to the American political system should certainly be monitored in every election, and that is precisely what AEI's *Public Opinion*

1

magazine did during the 1984 campaigns for the presidential nominations and election. Both of us were struck by the fact that the findings of many of the magazine's articles ran sharply counter to the conventional wisdom. They reported, for example, that:

- Paid political advertisements had almost *no* impact on the results of the Democratic presidential primaries.
- The candidate who spent the most on campaigning in a particular primary *lost* more often than the candidate who spent less.
- The network news programs showed almost *no* political bias on issues in their coverage of the general election campaign.
- American campaigns spend *less* per voter than those in most other democracies.
- The American people have *not* turned against the media in the mid-1980s.

Since we were surprised and impressed by many of these reports, we thought other media- and politics-watchers might be too. So we decided to put together a selection of articles and make it available as soon as possible. The result is this book.

The authors reflect the rich diversity of three distinct perspectives—journalism, politics, and academia. Nationally syndicated columnist Nick Thimmesch analyzes the print media. David Gergen, former director of communications in the Reagan White House, writes about the crisis of confidence in the media in the 1980s.

And William Adams, Stephen Bates, Maura Clancey, Edwin Diamond, Laurily Epstein, Barbara Farah, David Moore, Howard Penniman, Michael Robinson, and Gerald Strom, all academic students of the mass media and politics, put many of the leading scholarly theories to the test.

Each article presents new evidence on one or another of the main issues concerning the role of the media in presenting and shaping American politics, including:

- the special attention paid to the Iowa caucuses and the New Hampshire primary
- the techniques, cost, and impact of broadcast political advertising
- television coverage of the national party conventions
- the credibility of American journalism
- "liberal bias" in network news
- the power of television news to influence election outcomes
- the effects of early election-night projections of outcomes on late voting

While this is one of the first books to be published about the role of the media in the 1984 campaign, the foregoing issues and others it deals with are the ones that return election after election. Thus the articles' factual evidence and conclusions will have significance long after the 1984 election has receded into history.

PART ONE

Media in the Primaries and the Conventions

The Duration of Politics in New Hampshire

by David Moore

It is a tenet of faith among most reporters and political analysts these days that New Hampshire is a state where "retail politics," not "wholesale politics," is required for victory. Loosely translated, that means any candidate who expects to win—or even to do well—in the nation's first presidential primary must, as in the days of yore, engage in old fashioned, face-to-face campaigning: Contenders must knock on doors, talk with the people, and organize volunteer workers, rather than bombard voters with messages from afar via the mass media.

In the view of some observers, Gary Hart's upset victory in the 1984 New Hampshire primary only reinforces the notion that retail politics is crucial in the state: His campaign efforts and organization were generally rated among the two best there.

The notion is accepted by reporters and pundits as well as politicians, but it simply isn't true. If we look carefully at the 1984 campaign—and at earlier contests—we find very little evidence to support the myth.

Getting It Wholesale

In the 1984 primary campaign there were two major fluctuations in voter preferences: the first after Jesse Jackson's trip to Syria to secure the release of Lt. Robert Goodman and the second after the Iowa caucuses.

Jackson's late December trip was given a great deal of mostly favorable publicity, and although he barely campaigned in the state, he moved to the head of the "long-shot" candidate list following his mission. In the October University of New Hampshire (UNH) poll, he received only 1 percent in voter preference; by early February, he was at 8 percent. This surge was clearly a media surge.

The second major fluctuation occurred after the Iowa caucuses. According to ABC News/*Washington Post* polls, Gary Hart went from 12 percent to 30 percent in voter preferences, Mondale from 35 to 30 percent, and Glenn from 23 to 14 percent between February 18-20 and 25-27. The actual results were Hart 40, Mondale 29, and Glenn 13. Such large shifts had not occurred for anyone but Jackson between March 1983 and early 1984, despite extensive one-on-one campaigning. It is hardly plausible that local organizations or one-on-one campaigning caused these shifts within a one-week period. Clearly, the relentless media coverage of Hart's "better than expected" second place Iowa showing and Glenn's "very poor" showing there were key to the shifts in voter preference. Ironically, Mondale's organization was rated by many observers as the most extensive and the best financed in the state, yet Mondale's standing among voters dropped the most dramatically.

The importance of national media coverage is seen also in the 1980 election campaign. The UNH poll in February of 1979 showed Governor Jerry Brown of California acceptable to 49 percent of the voters as either their first or second choice (among Brown, Carter, and Kennedy). Six months later, in September, a UNH poll showed that figure had dropped to 28 percent, even though Brown was the only candidate to campaign to any significant extent during that period. Kennedy's acceptability jumped from 58 to 87 percent, though he had yet to declare his candidacy and had not started campaigning. This boost reflected the extensive (and generally positive) coverage he had received as he contemplated whether to challenge his party's incumbent president. Carter's rating dropped from 64 to 51 percent; he had not campaigned either.

Once Kennedy started campaigning, in October, his rating dropped. That reflected the nationwide reversal of Democratic opinions toward Kennedy and Carter. The Iranian hostage crisis worked to Carter's short-term political benefit, and Kennedy's comments about the Shah and his lackluster performance in an interview with Roger Mudd worked to his detriment. Without any personal campaigning in the state, Carter was able to beat Kennedy (and Brown) decisively in the primary, though those two candidates had campaigned extensively among the voters.

Table 1
WHAT HAPPENED IN NEW HAMPSHIRE?

	BG Dec. 10	UNH Jan. 29-Feb. 7	BG Jan. 31	BG Feb. 12-14	ABC/ WP Feb. 13-15	ABC/ WP Feb. 14-16	ABC/ WP Feb. 15-17	ABC/ WP Feb. 16-18	ABC/ WP Feb. 17-19
Mondale	45%	38%	42%	39%	42%	40%	37%	36%	34%
Glenn	19	17	19	18	21	18	18	16	20
Hart	6	7	8	10	10	12	15	18	17
Jackson	3	8	10	11	8	11	11	10	12
Sample size	(NA)	(507)	(NA)	(487)	(154)	(148)	(156)	(148)	(152)

Note: For *Boston Globe*, sample was Democrats and Independents. For University of New Hampshire, sample was Democrats and Democratic-leaning Independents. ABC/*Washington Post* sample was of registered Democrats and Independents who said they were certain to vote in the primary. Darden Research sample was of Democrats and Independents who said they were likely to vote in the primary. Teichner & Associates (WCVB) sample was of Democrats and Independents who planned to vote. NA = not available.

Thus, the dynamics of the 1980 New Hampshire Democratic primary were almost totally a function of national events reported in the national media, rather than the face-to-face campaigning for which the state is known.

Similarly, in the 1980 Republican primary, Bush's "emergence from the pack" came about not because of his campaigning in New Hampshire, but because of the media's wide coverage of his victory in Iowa, where Reagan had refused to campaign or participate in the debate. Bush's disastrous fall in New Hampshire was due to the Nashua debate only three days before the election. Television played the debate story over and over again. Reagan's confrontation with the moderator showed him a masterful leader and Bush a spoilsport. Until then, polls had shown a close race.

For both the 1980 and 1984 primaries, then, New Hampshire bore all the earmarks of a "media" state, where local campaigning did not prove to be as decisive in the electoral contest as did national media attention.

The Earlier Contests

A close examination of earlier contests shows that the myth of retail politics may not apply to them either. In 1968, Senator Eugene McCarthy's close second to President Johnson was probably not due to extensive organizing and campaigning in the state. McCarthy didn't declare his candidacy until January. Those who voted for him were a mixture of "hawks" and "doves" who opposed Johnson on the war either because they wanted the United States to be more aggressive or because they wanted an immediate withdrawal. They gravitated to McCarthy in a protest coalition made even more prominent by the TET offensive only a few weeks before the primary.

The 1972 primary seems to fit the "retail politics" model to some extent, because McGovern announced earlier and spent considerably more time and energy campaigning in New Hampshire than Senator Muskie did. But I suspect that if public opinion polls had been tracking the race closely, they would have revealed that Muskie's crying incident on the front steps of the *Manchester Union Leader* was far more devastating to his fortunes than McGovern's efforts were. McGovern, it should be recalled, still lost to Muskie by 9 points, and it is conceivable that, prior to that incident, Muskie's lead had been substantially greater than the final vote tally. We know from polls conducted in the 1980 race that the one incident of the Nashua debate resulted in Bush's loss and Reagan's gain of about 15 percentage points each, for a net difference at election time of almost 30 points.

If the crying incident caused even a 5 percentage point erosion in Muskie's vote (for a net gain to McGovern of 10 points) that alone may be responsible for starting the myth that one-on-one campaigning is key to success in New Hampshire. Without that incident, Muskie may have actually reached the "expected" 50 percent level or better (he received 46 percent) and beaten McGovern by 19-20 points. With those results, given the months of campaigning by McGovern, no one would have claimed that New Hampshire was especially sympathetic to long-shot candidates.

But then came 1976 and the emergence of Jimmy Carter. This solidified New Hampshire's image as the state where retail politics is essential for victory. A UNH poll conducted shortly before the election showed that Carter's campaign had contacted more potential voters than had Udall's, though the margin was only several percentage points. And, of course, Carter won by less than six points. Actually 1976 may meet the stereotype of retail politics because no candidate for the Democratic primary that year commanded special media attention. All were relatively unknown nationally. Although the Iowa caucuses were later identified as indicative of Carter's early strength, that contest was not given the media attention it received in 1980. The real attention of the media in 1976 began with the *results* of the New Hampshire primary election, not with earlier stages of the process.

But, of course, the Iowa caucuses will never again be slighted. Thus, whatever the presumed effect of retail politics in an earlier time, the New Hampshire primary today is dominated not by one-on-one campaigning, but by the nature of national media coverage. Certainly no candidate (White House incumbents may be an exception) can afford to be perceived as not doing his fair share of campaigning in any state. That image hurt Reagan in Iowa in 1980 and would hurt a candidate in New Hampshire as well. But barring such negative images, it does not follow that for a candidate to do well in New Hampshire, he must engage in *extensive* face-to-face campaigning, or that such campaigning will even help.

New Hampshire in that sense is similar to the rest of America, where wholesale politics is an unavoidable facet of electoral campaigns, and where one-on-one campaigning is simply not possible with the vast majority of voters. The myth of retail politics in New Hampshire may die hard, for many people would like to believe that it is so, and probably still will.   ☑

David Moore is an associate professor of political science at the University of New Hampshire and codirector of the New Hampshire poll.

Table 1
(continued)

ABC/ WP Feb. 18-20	ABC/ WP Feb. 19-21	ABC/ WP Feb. 20-22	WCVB Feb. 21-22	ABC/ WP Feb. 21-23	ABC/ WP Feb. 22-24	ABC/ WP Feb. 23-25	ABC/ WP Feb. 24-26	DRC/ CNN Feb. 25-26	ABC/ WP Feb. 25-27
35%	36%	37%	36%	39%	38%	38%	33%	38%	30%
23	22	18	13	14	14	14	16	15	14
12	12	16	9	22	24	24	26	32	14
12	14	11	7	9	7	6	8	7	8
(156)	(223)	(284)	(NA)	(343)	(351)	(349)	(341)	(500)	(446)

Source: Surveys by Harrison-Goldberg, Inc. for the *Boston Globe;* the University of New Hampshire; ABC News/*Washington Post;* Darden Research Corporation for Cable News Network; Teichner & Associates, Inc. for WCVB-TV and WHDH Radio.

by Michael J. Robinson

The Power of the Primary Purse: Money in 1984

"Money talks, bull---- walks." Former Congressman Michael Myers offered that theory of American politics into a hidden microphone just before accepting a bribe from an ABSCAM agent back in 1978.

Myers was merely expressing the conventional wisdom in unconventional English—that dollars equate with political power. But in contemporary presidential politics, the opposite may be true. It may be money that walks while something else does the talking.

Now that the primaries and caucuses are history, the FEC has released the final figures on who spent what, where, and when among the Democrats. If the state-by-state totals are accurate, they may prove that Mike Myers, and a whole lot of other people, have badly overstated the talking power of money. The FEC evidence suggests that he who spends more does not necessarily do better. Among Democrats in 1984, he who spent more generally did worse.

If one looks at *total* spending in the primary campaign, the first impression is that dollar politics works. In the aggregate, Walter Mondale, the winner, spent the most, just under $18 million. Gary Hart came in second in votes and in spending, with expenditures reaching just beyond $11 million. Jesse Jackson came in last among the three survivors and spent least, about $4.5 million.

But those aggregates mask what was really going on—more precisely what was *not* going on—among the several states. The relationship between money and voting disappears completely when we move from national spending totals to state totals.

The Democrats contested twenty-nine state and special primaries in 1984. In seventeen of those elections the person who won was not the biggest spender. In only ten instances did the most heavily bankrolled campaign receive a plurality of the vote. In the remaining two, spending levels were approximately equal.

Politically powerful New Hampshire usually gets bashed for being unrepresentative of the nation at large. But in this one respect New Hampshire and her primary were more than typical. John Glenn outspent everybody else in New Hampshire, and he came in a distant third. Hart spent about 25 percent less than Glenn, and Hart, of course, wound up the easy winner. And so it went throughout the winter and spring—losers had deep pockets, winners had shallow pockets.

With eight candidates in the race, it's almost impossible to make clean assessments. But within days after the New Hampshire primary the race came down to two men—Mondale and Hart. Their head-to-head campaign makes the case *against* the power of money even clearer.

Mondale and Hart were, in one way or another, on the ballot in all the states, though both campaigned selectively and strategically across the country. If we look only at the thirteen *major* contests—states in which both men actively campaigned and together spent half a million dollars or more—it is astounding to see what little effect money actually had.

These thirteen include all the turning points in the campaign: Iowa, New Hampshire, "Super Tuesday," Illinois, New York, Pennsylvania, Texas, Ohio, and "Final Tuesday." In eight of the thirteen, the campaign making the larger expenditures lost.

The table shows how much Hart and Mondale spent in each major state and includes the differences between them. A negative means that the loser spent more. A plus sign symbolizes that the winner spent more.

Table 1 EXPENDITURES			
State	**Gary Hart**	**Walter Mondale**	**Difference between winner and loser**
Iowa	$462,000	$654,000	+ $192,000
New Hampshire	345,000	402,000	− 57,000
Florida	691,000	475,000	+ 216,000
Alabama	222,000	374,000	+ 152,000
Georgia	442,000	367,000	− 75,000
Massachusetts	472,000	676,000	− 204,000
Illinois	577,000	312,000	− 265,000
New York	1,161,000	554,000	− 607,000
Pennsylvania	682,000	312,000	− 370,000
Texas	354,000	147,000	− 207,000
Ohio	396,000	185,000	+ 211,000
California	624,000	350,000	+ 274,000
New Jersey	854,000	368,000	− 486,000

In Georgia, a state that helped to save Mondale, Mondale spent $75,000 less than Hart—about 15 percent less. In Massachusetts, Hart's first industrial-state victory, Mondale outspent Hart by almost 50 percent.

Then came Illinois—the beginning of the end for Hart, but not for lack of spending. Hart pumped a quarter of a million dollars more into Illinois than did Mondale, only to slip fifteen points in the polls during the last few days of that campaign.

What happened next is even more telling. Within a fourteen-week period between early April and early May, New York, Pennsylvania, and Texas broke the neck of the Hart campaign. Mondale ran up pluralities of 17 percent in New York, 12 percent in Pennsylvania, and about 15 percent in Texas. But in every one of those three states, Hart outspent Mondale by *more than two to one*. In those three states alone, Hart spent $1.2 million more than his major opponent.

Part of this can be explained by the money that was spent on Mondale's behalf but that was not charged to him—money coming from Mondale's controversial delegate committees. Despite that qualification, money seemed to do for Hart in mid-spring what *The Right Stuff* had done for John Glenn last autumn—nothing, maybe less.

Even on "Final Tuesday," Hart saw just how little money can buy—this time in New Jersey, where Hart outspent Mondale by almost 250 percent and wound up capturing a meager 30 percent of the vote. In New Jersey Hart outspent Jesse Jackson almost 800 times over; yet Jackson got 24 percent of the vote.

Drunken Sailors

There are only five cases at best that imply the voters were sold a candidacy in 1984: Iowa, Florida, Alabama, Ohio, and California. But adding together all the spending in these major states, the total comes up negative. The losers outspent the winners in these critical states by about a million dollars. In short, money was not a very good investment in the caucuses and primaries.

The same thing happened with the Republicans in 1980. George Bush tended to win where he spent less and tended to lose when—compared with Reagan—he was the spendthrift. For the first two months of 1980, John Connally spent more quickly than any of his opponents. Never has one candidate spent so much, so fast, and purchased so little—$13 million for one delegate.

This year's pattern of expenditures and voting outcomes suggests that money not only fails to help, but may harm candidates. The negative correlation does not imply—let alone prove—that well-heeled candidates and campaigns will always lose. Nor does this correlation imply simply that candidates spend more when behind. What the negative relationship really means is that, first, *candidates spend money whenever they have it to spend*; second, *what they spend has little relationship to outcome*.

When Mondale had big bucks, he spent big bucks —and, for reasons not directly related, he lost. The same holds true for Hart. Hart had modest amounts of money in January, so he spent modestly. After his better-than-expected finish in Iowa, he increased his daily campaign contributions by a factor of six. After his honest-to-goodness victory in New Hampshire, Hart was collecting upwards of $100,000 per day—money he then spent while he was botching up his "real" campaign. In the end, Hart had to learn that what one spends on a presidential campaign is far less important than how one conducts oneself day to day.

The Denatured Dollar

Money did matter once upon a time, or at least it seems so. If that's true, why has it lost its value in today's presidential nominations? The first reason is obvious. Election laws mean that nobody can outspend an opponent by much in any given race, because nobody is *allowed* to spend much in any given race. Nobody has spent millions of dollars in New Hampshire, or any other state, because it is, in a phrase, against the law to do so. Consequently, the relative dollar differences between candidates are nowhere near as great as they used to be.

Second, as long as a candidate can spend a reasonable fraction of what the opponents are spending, the advantage of money is neutralized. All that really matters is that candidates are able to spend enough money to be visible. Jesse Jackson provides the best example of how far one can go on a pittance.

Third, and related to the last point, is that forces outside the candidate's control overshadow the "paid" parts of presidential campaigns—even paid advertising, one of the biggest budget items. The average American child grows up with 10,000 television commercials per year. By the time he or she becomes an average American voter, he or she is well beyond the point at which commercials could determine a presidential preference. And, if you think not, look back at the figures on expenditures and outcomes over the last three presidential campaigns.

The Way You Play the Game

If money doesn't talk, what does? In 1984, we saw how important the most basic elements of politics can be: demographics, for example.

With Jackson in the campaign, the correlation between a state's racial composition and the caucus or primary outcome was dramatic. And just as race proved to be a major factor in voting, so did region. Hart won in the West regardless of how much he spent. Mondale won in the midwestern states that were most like his own.

Even big-shot endorsements correlated more closely with victory than money did. Governor Mario Cuomo was obviously worth more to Mondale in New York than the $600,000 advantage Gary Hart bought for himself in that state. Organization counted, too—though less than most had originally expected. But organization is so closely related to money, one could argue that money does matter—not so much for the ads that it buys but for the lawyers and staff that it helps to pay.

Perhaps. But lawyers and staff are not generally what one means by dollar politics. Those services cost very little when compared with the price of pollsters, paid media advisers, and high-tech consultants.

It may go too far to say that candidates win presidential nominations the old-fashioned way—that they earn them instead of buy them. These days, they win or lose mostly on how well they play the "free" media game—in debates, on talk shows, in the local press, and above all, during the evening news.

Hart is the classic case. Hart lost the nomination because he messed up his free media performance after his New England miracle—proving to voters in Illinois and New York that he was neither predictable nor mature enough to be president. At the very moment that his paid campaign was raising and spending millions, Hart's free media campaign was doing him in.

So why do candidates spend so much time and money raising money? First, politicians who aspire to the presidency have psyches that render them vulnerable to anybody who says "with enough money and the right advertising I can make you President of the United States." To paraphrase H. L. Mencken, no political consultant ever went broke overestimating the ego of an American politician.

Second, presidential politicians usually start by campaigning in congressional or gubernatorial races, both of which—for a host of reasons—are the types of elections in which money does talk. Third, national politicians believe—probably rightly—that nobody ever spent himself *out* of a presidential nomination. Besides, what else is there to do other than raise and spend money? Fourth, they raise money for the same reason that the superpowers build weapons systems: because everybody else does.

Fifth, they play dollar politics because raising and spending money has become a bizarre test of the seriousness of a candidacy. He who first qualifies for matching funds seems most "serious." He who files penny-ante reports with the FEC looks like a prospective loser. Since 1980, campaign money has been raised not merely to impress voters through advertising but, instead, to impress journalists and opponents with the legitimacy of one's campaign. Thus, the classic irony: campaign money for money's sake.

Sergio Bendixen, campaign manager for Alan Cranston, carried the money game farther than most. At the beginning of 1984, Bendixen campaigned against Gary Hart by pointing out continuously how badly Hart was doing with his fund raising. Part of the reason the press missed the Hart story was that the Cranston people kept using FEC reports to dismiss Hart and hype Cranston to a degree completely unwarranted by poll-based reality.

The bad news about all this is that presidential candidates probably invest much more time in money politics than recent campaign history would indicate. Some might even be offended if they knew that political consultants and paid media advisers are growing rich preying upon the egocentric fantasies of middle-age politicians.

But then there's the unmistakable good news. Congressman Mike Myers was wrong. And so are the committed cynics and professional reformers who insist that money is becoming more important in national presidential politics.

The people may not know much about the issues. They may be increasingly impressed by looks and style alone, and less impressed with substance. Nonetheless, they do not buy nominees the way they buy soap. In the last analysis, although money may still be the root of all evil, it is quite clearly not a very effective route to the contemporary White House. ☞

Michael Robinson *is a visiting scholar at AEI and director of the Media Analysis Project at AEI and George Washington University.*

by William C. Adams

Media Coverage of Campaign '84: A Preliminary Report

The audiences of mass media apparently sub-scribe to the circular belief: "If you really matter, you will be at the focus of mass attention and, if you are at the focus of mass attention, then surely you must really matter."

Paul Lazarsfeld and Robert Merton, 1948

On February 20th, 1984, a few thousand Iowa Democrats and a few hundred leading journalists elevated Senator Gary Hart to the status of a leading contender for the Democratic nomination. From that evening forward Hart was granted the credibility and media attention he had been denied throughout 1983. One week later, Hart demolished Walter Mondale in the New Hampshire primary. What role did the news media play and when did they play it?

Poll-Based Media

As 1983 began, those who were high in the polls were those who had received the most prior media attention —Walter Mondale (former vice-president), John Glenn (former astronaut), and George McGovern (former Democratic nominee). A December 1982 Gallup survey showed that most people had learned the lessons of past headlines and knew Mondale (86 percent), Glenn (69 percent), and McGovern (73 percent). These same three men topped the early list of preferred Democratic nominees.

The survey also showed that fewer than one-third had ever heard of Alan Cranston (30 percent), Gary Hart (22 percent), Reubin Askew (23 percent), or Ernest Hollings (15 percent). Each of these four candidates was named as the preferred nominee by no more than 2 percent of the Democrats polled.

Subsequent news attention throughout 1983 was apportioned so that it almost perfectly paralleled candidate standings in the polls. As shown in table 1, rankings of the volume of coverage on the nightly network news and stories in both the *Washington Post* and *New York Times* followed symmetrically the early candidate standings in the polls.

George McGovern did not announce until October of 1983 and was the only candidate to end the year with any discrepancy between his poll ranking and news ranking. Jesse Jackson also decided to run late in the year, but he had enjoyed considerable coverage with pre-announcement speculation about his candidacy.

Table 1
RANKINGS IN POLLS AND 1983 COVERAGE

	Dec. '82 Gallup	'83 TV time	'83 Post & Times stories	Dec. '83 Gallup
Mondale	1 (32%)	1	1	1 (40%)
Glenn	2 (14)	2	2	2 (24)
Jackson	– –	3	3	3 (10)
McGovern	3 (6)	8	7	4 (8)
Hart	4 (2)	4	4	5 (3)
Cranston	4 (2)	5	5	5 (3)
Hollings	4 (2)	6	5	7 (2)
Askew	7 (1)	7	8	8 (1)

The 1983 allocations of coverage let the rich get richer. As shown in table 1, the only candidates to improve significantly in the polls during 1983 were those who had dominated print and broadcast journalism—Walter Mondale and John Glenn. (There are no baseline data on Jackson, but his pattern is consistent with this finding.) Conversely, those who were poll poor at the start stayed media poor through most of the year. Having failed to become the "focus of mass attention," they did not "really matter."

Media-Based Polls

Journalists did more than just follow the lead of poll standings in 1983 by continuing to reinforce the pre-existing pecking order. They also independently contributed to poll shifts.

Most of the poll fluctuations in 1983 were trivial, well within the range of ordinary sampling error. There were, however, four statistically prominent surges in Gallup polls of Democrats during 1983: John Glenn's ratings shot up between mid-March and the end of April; both Walter Mondale's and Alan Cranston's ratings improved between the end of April and mid-June; and Mondale's ratings jumped between mid-October and mid-November.

Each of these notable gains immediately followed a surge in the combined attention of television, newspapers, and news magazines. For example, Glenn's spring gains came just after he announced his candidacy and obtained favorable profiles in news magazines and elsewhere. Cranston's early summer boost came in the wake of media interest in his Wisconsin straw poll victory and his leadership on the nuclear freeze issue.

In only one instance did major media attention fail to boost a candidate in the polls in 1983: "The Right Stuff" generated enormous press interest. For the first time, a movie lionizing the heroics of a presidential candidate was being released on the eve of the primary campaign. The actor who played astronaut John Glenn was featured on the cover of *Newsweek*.

The October hoopla about "The Right Stuff" brought no gains to Glenn in subsequent polls. Except for this instance, however, periods of relatively intense media attention were followed by upturns for the beneficiary in the next Gallup poll.

The overall pattern is interactive: Prior visibility begets high poll ratings which beget media coverage/legitimacy which begets improved poll standings which beget media coverage/legitimacy. For those with little initial standing, the pattern is fairly stable. Low visibility begets under 5 percent in the polls which begets little media attention/credibility which begets continued low standings in the polls. In every phase, the poll-media cycle depresses or stimulates the other two key elements in campaign dynamics: money and volunteers. The next stage, however, exhibits a radical transformation.

Iowa-Based Media

As soon as the primary and caucus season begins, journalists take an altogether different perspective on the nomination race. They abandon reliance on national polls to rank the candidates. Instead, for the first month, the pecking order is set by the results of the last caucus and primary—no matter how small and unrepresentative they may be. The rollercoaster or juggernaut begins.

To measure the relative attention devoted to the candidates, this researcher analyzed weeknight CBS and NBC newscasts from February 13 (one week before the Iowa caucuses) through March 13 (Super Tuesday). Among the variables coded were the amounts of airtime devoted to each Democratic candidate. Calculated as a percent of the total time given to all Democratic candidates, this measure tells us the relative share of attention assigned to each candidate.

During the week before the Iowa caucuses, airtime allocations still mirrored national polls, with Mondale way out front, and Glenn and Jackson coming in second and third. Most of the rest of the pack were essentially ignored. Hart received 4 percent of the candidate coverage that week, as did McGovern. Hollings and Askew each received less than 2 percent.

The Iowa caucuses changed all of that. On February 20, about 85,000 people attended the Democratic caucuses—*that is less than one-sixth of the people who regularly vote Democratic in presidential elections in Iowa*. In other words, total caucus turnout constituted no more than 17 percent of the half-million Iowa Democratic votes cast in 1972, for example, for McGovern.

This one-sixth segment of the party resides in a state that has gone Democratic only once since siding with neighbor Harry Truman in 1948. Iowa Democrats may be impotent when November rolls around, but, thanks to the news, in February they dwarf Democrats everywhere.

The networks direct enormous attention to these first caucuses—often devoting over one-third of the entire newscast to the race. For the many voters who are just waking up to the contest, these initial Iowa images are crucial.

Although no candidate came close to Mondale's 45 percent of the vote, measured against expectations, three surprises emerged from Iowa: (1) Glenn did quite poorly, with only 5 percent; (2) Hart unexpectedly came in second, though he had only 15 percent (12,600 votes); and (3) McGovern came in a startling third with 13 percent (10,700 votes)—less than 2,000 votes behind Hart.

Despite the tiny size of the electorate, the media verdict was unequivocal, and the self-fulfilling power attributed to the caucuses was monumental:

> Senators Hart and Glenn traded places in Iowa. Hart moved up to number two. Glenn became an also-ran. The effect of this surprising reversal already is being felt in their campaigns.
> —Tom Brokaw, NBC News, February 21, 1984.

Iowa produced some far-reaching transformations of news priorities. Ostensibly, Mondale was given his due: "number one by far" (Dan Rather, CBS, February 20); "a big victory for the front-runner" (Tom Brokaw, NBC, February 21). *In the week following his Iowa triumph, however, Mondale actually suffered a decline in his relative share of attention on CBS and NBC newscasts.*

Mondale's relative standing was diminished because broadcast journalists awarded newfound status to Gary Hart and drafted preliminary obituaries for John Glenn. Hart gained and Mondale suffered most on NBC, where Hart's airtime actually equalled that of Mondale after Iowa—each received almost 30 percent of candidate airtime (see figure 1). Though not quite so dramatically, Hart also gained at Mondale's expense on CBS.

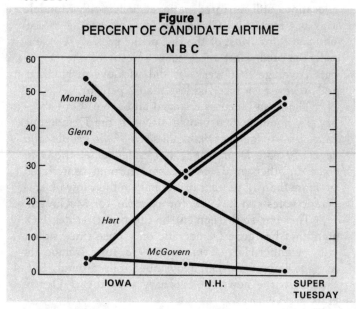

Figure 1
PERCENT OF CANDIDATE AIRTIME
N B C

Hart's relative share of coverage the week after Iowa was ten times what it had been the week before on NBC and five times what it had been on CBS. In the meantime, viewers were told that Iowa was almost fatal for Glenn who "tried to put on a brave front" and whose new goal was "simply surviving" (NBC), hoping for "some emergency oxygen for his badly shaken campaign" (CBS).

One of the curious twists of news coverage was that George McGovern profited not at all from his unanticipated third place in Iowa. McGovern finished close behind Hart, but he did not come close to getting Hart's bonanza of coverage. *McGovern obtained even less coverage, proportionately, after Iowa than before it.* Following Iowa, less than 4 percent of the nightly candidate airtime on CBS and NBC went to McGovern —a tiny fraction of that bestowed on Hart.

Why was McGovern given this peculiar treatment? It may be that the top two Iowa "shocks" (Glenn and Hart) displaced time for the third (McGovern). One other possibility is the perceptual screen of journalists who could not accept McGovern as a serious contender. In either event, the Iowa criterion used to reorder the rest of the lineup was not applied in Mc-Govern's case.

Taken together, the Iowa "surprises" raise another issue. Some might argue that the Iowa outcome really refutes the entire theory that the media confer status—after all, Glenn did far worse, while Hart and McGovern did better, than national media coverage would have predicted. Actually, Iowa only demonstra-

ted (via John Glenn) that prior media attention alone does not guarantee a constituency but only offers an opportunity to assemble one; it does not indefinitely compensate for weak speeches and poor organization.

Iowa also demonstrated that it is still possible for a candidate (Gary Hart) who journalists treat as a dark horse to mobilize 3 percent (12,600) of the Iowans who regularly vote Democratic in presidential elections (500,000) to attend caucuses one evening in February. That little feat forces us not to demolish but only to qualify notions of media status conferral when it comes to small subsets of activists early in a presidential campaign.

At the same time that Hart's coverage soared, there was some restraint. For example, CBS's Bruce Morton observed (February 21):

It's probably worth reminding ourselves, though, that he [Hart] was after all a distant second. This is not a George McGovern in 1972 coming quite close to Ed Muskie. Now, when you lose three-to-one, you've lost.

Yet despite such occasional comments, two things happened after February 20th: Hart was presented as the leading alternative to Walter Mondale, and Hart's coverage was virtually free of any harsh criticism, unflattering issues, or cynical commentary.

John Glenn was "trying desperately to recharge his batteries" (Brokaw), and Jesse Jackson was "spending a lot of time . . . defensively fielding questions about . . . alleged remarks about Jews" (Rather). McGovern continued to be neglected, and the rest hardly existed in the world of the networks. This left Gary Hart enjoying his Iowa windfall of coverage, exempt from attacks by Mondale (who was ironically attacking Reagan for "amnesia"), and not yet ripe for network inquiries into his name, age, and "new ideas."

On February 28th, Hart beat Mondale by one of the largest margins ever recorded for the winner of a contested New Hampshire Democratic primary.

New Hampshire-Based Media

The unrepresentativeness of New Hampshire is always noted—without, however, seriously minimizing the imputed importance of the primary's outcome. Unlike the Iowa caucuses, the New Hampshire primary does draw as many as two-thirds of the people who vote Democratic in November. Their numbers are still small, however; New Hampshire has gone Democratic only once since the presidential election of 1944.

Following Hart's triumph in New Hampshire, CBS and NBC presented viewers with a two-man race. In the two weeks following New Hampshire, Glenn, with 4 percent of the candidate airtime on CBS and 7 percent on NBC, joined McGovern (5 percent on CBS and 1 percent on NBC) in relative obscurity. Askew, Cranston, and Hollings finally got some coverage when they dropped out of the race.

Hart's free ride from both Mondale and the media

eventually came to an end. His relatively undamaged image began to suffer some attacks.

On March 2, viewers heard for the first time on NBC some sustained criticisms of Gary Hart. That same evening, CBS also began its ventures into critiquing Gary Hart. "Now there are two front-runners," as Bob Simon put it, so it was time for Hart to start taking his medicine.

These scripts offered the serious opening volleys of the classic "attack the front-runner" mode that Michael Robinson and Margaret Sheehan documented so well for the 1980 campaign in *Over the Wire and On TV*. Gary Hart, CBS suggested, mimics John Kennedy. Simon termed Hart "trendy." Not devastating perhaps, but it was a start.

After the digression of Hart's nonbinding win in Vermont, CBS began to pick up steam. Bruce Morton on March 8:

Gary Hart is the hottest political property around —at least this week. . . .
Hart's fundamental theme is newness, even though he is just nine years younger than Walter Mondale. . . .
Newness hasn't stopped Hart from sometimes courting older politicians like George Wallace. . . .
His invocation of the Kennedys is deliberate. . . .
Hart has made some proposals . . . but his proposals often don't get as far as the Senate floor. . . .

After Morton finished, Rather read a long studio story about "the touchy question of Senator Hart's age."

Investigative journalism surfaced at about the same time at NBC. On March 9th, NBC featured a major report on Hart's name and age. Both networks, however, saved their strongest salvos for the evening before Super Tuesday.

Super Monday

Monday, March 12, was the last nightly newscast before Super Tuesday's primaries in Alabama, Georgia, Florida, Massachusetts, and Rhode Island, plus caucuses in four Western states. That evening all three networks ran a succession of stories hitting Gary Hart's credibility and image. A summary of that evening's stories illustrates the vigor of the new scrutiny of the new front-runner. ABC, not included in our monitoring, is used here for comparison purposes.

CBS led with a long story that firmly refuted Hart's versions of what he had once said about Cuba and then rejected Hart's interpretation of something he once told the National Women's Political Caucus. The next story focused on interviews with two elderly Florida men whose uninformed support of Hart was based on "his personal style."

After the commercial, viewers heard Senator Glenn ("his battered campaign limped into the South") attacking Senator Hart. And at a Massachusetts rally ("maybe a last hurrah") for McGovern, it was explained that "privately McGovern has expressed deep reservations about Gary Hart." CBS viewers that eve-

ning could easily conclude that McGovern's reservations were justified.

ABC led its newscast with an "issue" piece in which Barry Serafin concluded, "In short, it is chemistry and tone, not issues, that appear to be governing the hot new Democratic race." Then came Jack Smith's examination of Hart, looking "beyond the slogans."

What Smith found was a "foundering, poorly managed, and unfocused" campaign until Pat Caddell "provided the packaging Hart badly needed." Smith explained that Hart "is not ashamed of exploiting the clichés" of Kennedy. "By all accounts, though, Hart lacks the Kennedy charm." Shockingly, Hart is "also very ambitious; some who know him say he is driven by it."

Warming to the subject, Smith noted "Hart's moves have sometimes appeared calculated," and reviewed Hart's efforts to acquire "the military record missing from his resumé" and the politically convenient reconciliation with his wife. He went on to list Hart's changes of his religion, his name, his age, and even his signature.

Smith referred to Hart's often unsuccessful record in the Senate, and concluded pointedly that "voters have yet to take their measure of the man—surveys show his momentum so far has been built more on style than content." Voters who judged Hart based on ABC's sketch could not have found a very attractive figure.

That same evening, NBC joined ABC and CBS in their biting and one-sided critiques of Hart—thus creating the kind of astonishing pack journalism that excites conspiracy theorists, outrages those who value diversity, and fascinates content analysts. NBC ran a particularly rough series of stories and quotations about Hart the evening before Super Tuesday. Included were attacks on Hart from Claude Pepper, Walter Mondale, John Glenn, and Richard Viguerie.

Reporter Lisa Myers began: "A noticeably more upbeat Mondale stormed across the South, sounding his new battle cry." Mondale: "Where's the beef? Where's the beef?" Then she introduced "the political patron saint of social security" (Claude Pepper) who offered the unchallenged assertion that Hart wants to cut social security benefits. Next, Mondale was shown questioning Hart's "uncertainty" and "inconsistency."

A few minutes later in a John Dancy story, two friends variously characterized Hart as "basically moderate" (William Cohen) or "liberal" (Leon Shull). But then Richard Viguerie called him a "1980s version of George McGovern" who has been "very clever to package himself" as a nonliberal.

Turning to another perspective, the audience was told about Virginia Volker, a college professor and member of N.O.W., who was said to be "worried about the Gary Hart surge, and a little resentful." Tom Brokaw suggested to her: "Mondale is not a fad, and you believe Gary Hart is."

One citizen for Hart was interviewed that evening. She conceded she leaned toward Hart because she liked "that image," even though "it may not be the best reason to vote for someone." Brokaw wanted to pursue that subject:

Brokaw: Felice, Mondale says that Gary Hart has no new ideas, that he has no experience, that he's just riding the crest of his popularity. Do you stop and think about that?

Felice admitted "that was probably the issue that bothered me most." On that important NBC newscast, Hart was not once shown defending himself or uttering a single word.

The next day, Gary Hart did win in New England and Florida, and in the caucus states. Mondale, however, was victorious in Alabama and Georgia.

The Day Before

A funny thing happened just before Super Tuesday. It seems that people who made up their minds on the eve of the primary were far less likely to favor Hart than were those who had decided soon after New Hampshire. (It may of course have been just a coincidence that had nothing to do with the blasts from the networks.)

Table 2
WHEN VOTE WAS DECIDED
(CBS/NYT Super Tuesday Exit Polls)

	Last 3 days	After N.H.	Earlier this year	Knew all along
ALABAMA:				
Hart	33%	61%	28%	6%
Mondale	26	11	35	47
Others	41	28	37	47
GEORGIA:				
Hart	35%	72%	24%	8%
Mondale	25	14	28	48
Others	40	14	48	44
MASSACHUSETTS:				
Hart	37%	77%	45%	20%
Mondale	20	8	22	37
Others	43	15	33	43

The CBS/*New York Times* analysis summarized the exit poll findings this way:

There were indications in the South that the incredible momentum favoring Gary Hart had at least slowed down. Voters in Alabama who made up their minds between the New Hampshire primary and the Sunday before Super Tuesday voted for Gary Hart over Walter Mondale by a margin close to 6 to 1.

However, support for Mondale and Hart was much more evenly divided among those voters who made up their minds in the 3 days before the primary.

Hart's ratio over Mondale shrank from 6 to 1 (among those deciding during the post-New Hampshire honeymoon) to 4 to 3 (among Alabamans making their choice during the late period of harsh coverage). They found

the same pattern in the other two states where they conducted exit polls (see table 2).

In Georgia, almost three-fourths of those who decided soon after New Hampshire went for Hart. Yet, only one-third of those who decided "in the last three days" preferred Hart. Likewise, in Massachusetts, nearly 8 out of 10 of those deciding after New Hampshire favored Hart. Among those deciding when the network honeymoon was over, only 4 out of 10 chose Hart. In all three states, Mondale—as well as Jackson, McGovern, and Glenn—did markedly better among those who made up their minds just before Super Tuesday than among those who decided after New Hampshire.

Power and Status Conferral

Coverage of the race for the Democratic nomination ought to force second thoughts on those who habitually dismiss any theory of overt media political power. All of the available evidence indicates that the race was fundamentally influenced from 1983 onward by news media choices:

- The choice to cast the 1983 roles using survey results—helping Mondale and Glenn.
- The choice to restructure the entire race in 1984 based on the views of one-sixth of the Democrats in Iowa—helping Hart and hurting Glenn, Cranston, Askew, and Hollings.
- The choice to anoint a new major candidate based on the views of 3 percent of the Democrats in Iowa—helping Hart enormously.
- The choice to postpone serious criticism of the newly elevated candidate—helping Hart.
- The choice not to elevate another candidate who fared nearly as well in Iowa and thus the choice to apply the results of Iowa selectively—hurting McGovern.
- The choice to treat the cumulative verdict of Democrats in Iowa and New Hampshire as decisive tests—helping Hart and damaging the rest.
- The choice of whether, when, and how to initiate critical investigative reports on a candidate—hurting Hart starting about March 8-12.

In every instance these media content changes were followed by changes in public opinion.

There is no easy and obvious way to apportion campaign attention. These decisions and choices are invariably difficult. Yet their exercise can cause profound swings in public opinion, especially when they involve candidates about whom the public has yet to form stable opinions. That journalists must make such decisions is unavoidable—but that does not make their decisions any less powerful or any less influential. The power to confer status and mold images does determine, to echo Lazarsfeld and Merton, who "really matters." ☑

William C. Adams *is an associate professor of public administration at George Washington University.*

by Barbara G. Farah

Delegate Polls: 1944 to 1984

Polling delegates became a big business in 1984. The three television networks, the wire services, some of the print media, and at least two private organizations (the National Women's Political Caucus and the LTV Corporation) launched major operations to poll these individuals. For the media, delegate surveys had once been considered a luxury. In 1984's competitive media market, they had become a necessity.

Most of this year's delegates, Democratic and Republican, had anticipated neither the frequency of polling nor the comprehensiveness of the questions they would be expected to answer. Democratic delegates were polled more heavily than their Republican counterparts for the obvious reason that the Democratic nomination contest was close. Each of the Democratic delegates received about a dozen telephone calls from the media pollsters, some lasting as long as fifty-five minutes.

The networks pursued the delegates relentlessly, often beginning the efforts months before the conventions. Democrats reported being tracked down at their summer homes, their relatives' dinner tables, business conferences, and their vacation spots in the United States and abroad. By the time they reached San Francisco and Dallas, the Democrats and Republicans had learned to respond almost automatically to questions concerning their presidential and vice presidential choices and their views on economic, social, and foreign policy issues. An array of demographic details completed the picture.

Given the extent of this year's efforts, it is hard to believe that *no* network delegate surveys were taken before 1968. Before that, non-systematic delegate counts based largely on conversations with the candidates and state party chairmen provided the networks the information they needed.

In 1968, CBS News established the first media delegate poll. Martin Plissner, who designed the poll, recalls that he wanted to survey the delegates, not only to ascertain their choices for vice president and president in a systematic way, but also to be able to provide reporters with detailed information about the individual delegates. By doing this, CBS's coverage would be different from that of the other networks.

CBS's new venture had an unexpected effect for the network in 1968. That year the network had learned from its survey that Richard Nixon was leading by only a few delegate votes. They also learned that Nixon's support among southern delegates was "soft." Indeed, their poll hinted that a Reagan upset was possible. This information made CBS News more cautious than the other two networks in projecting an early winner. The 1968 poll also provided some valuable information for the Democratic party. The McGovern-Fraser commission was set up in 1968 to reform the party rules. Although the party knew that the proportion of women, blacks, young people, and other minorities represented among the delegates was low, the 1968 survey results showed them how poorly represented these groups were. They also made it possible to compare the Democrats to the Republicans. In 1968, for example, only 13 percent of the Democratic delegates were women, in contrast to 17 percent in the Republican party.

CBS News remained virtually alone in its polling effort for the next three presidential election years. Other media made limited attempts to poll delegates, but only CBS News could claim to have reached over 90 percent of the delegates in each of these years. Between 1972 and 1984, the network expanded its polls to include more questions on issues. The network also introduced comparisons of delegates and party rank and file, through the CBS News/*New York Times* surveys.

The areas covered by the 1984 surveys were strikingly similar. The vice presidential choice was a major topic in the Democratic delegate polls. Though most polls compared the opinions of Mondale, Hart, and Jackson supporters on this and other questions, the *New York Times* varied the theme by focusing on the opinions and preferences of delegates and the superdelegates. The *Times* found that Mondale's support came disproportionately from the superdelegates.

Republican delegates were the subjects of fewer polls because the contest outcome was so certain. But the media that did poll the Republicans all noticed a predominance of delegates who considered themselves ideologically conservative.

The Academic Angle

Scholars discovered convention delegates several decades ago, long before the media did. Academic surveys have been more limited, however, focusing on one party, or one state, or a subset of delegates. The one exception is a 1956 survey of convention delegates, conducted by Herbert McClosky and his colleagues, which explored how representative the delegates were of party rank and file. McClosky and his colleagues concluded that Democratic elites were closer ideologically to both the Democratic and the Republican rank and file than the Republican elites were to their own party identifiers.

This same theme has been echoed in subsequent studies of convention delegates and seemed particularly appealing in the reform politics era. Jeane Kirkpatrick, currently ambassador to the United Nations, argued in *The New Presidential Elite*, a book based on surveys of the 1972 delegates, that Democratic reform politics had exaggerated the differences between the Democratic leaders and their rank and file and consequently had made the Republican leaders appear more in tune with the issue positions of the Democratic electorate. By 1976, John Jackson and his research team at the University of Michigan had found that the dominance of Democratic moderates at the convention that year had helped to reestablish the usual symmetry between partisan leaders and their followers.

A study of 1980 convention delegates and their rank and file conducted by Warren E. Miller, M. Kent Jennings, and myself, indicated that the Republican leadership was, as it had been in 1956, out of step with the ideological preferences of their followers. The Democratic party leaders held issue positions closer to those of their own rank and file as well as to those held

Table 1

DELEGATE SURVEYS: FORTY YEARS APART

	1944 Dem.	1944 Rep.	1968 Dem.	1968 Rep.	1976 Dem.	1976 Rep.	1984** Dem.	1984** Rep.
By Sex:								
Men	89%	91%	87%	83%	67%	69%	49%	54%
Women	11	9	13	17	33	31	51	46
By Education:								
High school or less	24	23	NA	NA	NA	NA	11	12
Some college	18	18	NA	NA	NA	NA	18	25
College grad	12	16	19	—	21	27	20	28
More than college degree	46	41	44	34	43	38	51	35
Average age (in years)	52	54	49	49	43	48	44	51
By Occupation:								
Lawyer	38	37	28	22	16	15	17	14
Union leader	2	—	4	—	6	—	6	—
Executive	9	10	27	40	17	30	14	26
Other profession/teacher	24	35	8	2	26	12	36	27
Public official	11	6	13	13	12	9	9	6
Housewife	6	5	*	*	7	15	4	13
Never attended convention before	63	63	67	66	80	78	74	69
By Ideology:								
Liberal	*	*	*	*	40	3	50	1
Moderate	*	*	*	*	47	45	42	35
Conservative	*	*	*	*	8	48	5	60

Note: *Questions not asked in these years. **1984 figures are a combination of the CBS News poll, the *New York Times* poll and the *Los Angeles Times* poll; the 1968 and 1976 figures come from the CBS News poll. The occupation categories are not exactly the same for the 1944 study and the later polls. That will explain the discrepancy between "executive" in the early year and the later ones.

by the Republican electorate. This apparent incompatibility did little to hinder either Ronald Reagan's election that year or the support he received from a sizable number of Democrats. From what media polls have already shown about the 1984 delegates, this asymmetrical pattern once again exists between Republican leaders and their followers.

For political scientists, the 1968 Democratic convention was a watershed. The party's efforts to institute reforms at the 1972 convention rekindled interest in the delegate elites. Researchers descended on Miami Beach that year in droves to interview delegates and to observe the convention proceedings.

That same year, the Center for Political Studies at the University of Michigan initiated the most comprehensive survey of delegates, co-sponsored by the Russell Sage Foundation and the Twentieth Century Fund. From this survey, Jeane Kirkpatrick documented the emergence of a "new breed" of Democratic delegates, who defined themselves more in terms of the candidates they supported than in terms of traditional party values or issues.

The Michigan-based delegate research project entered a new phase in 1980. Russell Sage again sponsored the study, in which researchers reinterviewed 1972 delegates and interviewed 1976 and 1980 delegates for the first time. We charted the movements of these party elites in and out of presidential politics. We were also interested in the continuity of their participation. We documented two major trends: the ascendancy of conservatism in the Republican party over the last decade, and women's emergence as a powerful force in national party politics. The Michigan research enterprise will continue with its 1984 study. In addition, a consortium

of scholars from academic institutions across the nation have also been studying delegates to state conventions since 1980. Ronald Rappaport, Alan Abramowitz, and Walter Stone, who are involved in this project, are examining the candidate preference ordering of delegates to better understand the decision-making process among party elites. John Jackson and his group of scholars continue to examine issue similarities and differences between rank and file and convention delegates, and among state party chairs and national committee members.

Another scholar who has been studying convention delegates since at least 1968 is Byron Shafer. Unlike other researchers, who are interested in delegates as party activists, Shafer is concerned with party conventions as political institutions.

The Simple Past

Now that complex convention delegate surveys are so prevalent, it is difficult to imagine what we did without them. Back in 1944, delegates to both conventions received a questionnaire on a penny postcard from a young Northwestern University assistant professor. It asked only eight questions: state, age, occupation, education, previous convention attended, and party and public officeholding experience.

Once the data were collected, they were tucked away in Professor LeRoy Ferguson's office, where they stayed until his retirement forty years later. The yellowed cards, stuffed in two large dusty shoeboxes, were then turned over to the Center for Political Studies at the University of Michigan.

Much to the delight of the graduate student designated to code the information on the 1,059 Republican and 1,176 Democratic delegates, the shoeboxes yielded responses from a few notables. From the Republican party came Hollywood movie producer Cecil B. deMille and a young political novice from Minnesota, Warren Burger. The latter, having no party or public officeholding experience to report, indicated on the card that he had "no personal political ambition" beyond supporting his party's platform and ticket, and serving as one of Governor Harold Stassen's floor whips at the convention.

On the Democratic side, incumbent Vice President Henry Wallace attended the convention as a delegate, only to find that he would not be renominated as Franklin D. Roosevelt's fourth term running mate. Two of the younger Democratic delegates attending that year's convention were Edmund G. Brown, Sr. from California, who had recently switched his party allegiance, and Hubert H. Humphrey from Minnesota, already an active member of his state's Democratic Farm Labor party.

The 1944 study reminds us that convention delegate polling—today a national pastime—had humble beginnings. ☑

Barbara G. Farah is director of news surveys at the New York Times.

by William C. Adams

Convention Coverage

The last CBS News/*New York Times* poll before the San Francisco convention disclosed something startling: Just 61 percent of the Democratic rank-and-file said they intended to vote for Walter Mondale.

CBS News/*New York Times* summer polls also demonstrated that most people believed the country was better off than it had been four years earlier, and most people attributed that to the economic surge and the easing of inflation. When asked about the country's "most important problem," economic issues far surpassed everything else.

During the many hours of prime-time convention coverage, these two pivotal stories—the defection of Democratic regulars and the political effect of the economic boom—were given little attention by two giants of the American news media—CBS News and NBC

News. These omissions were puzzling because convention coverage was so extensive.

Convention Significance

Conventions offer the largest dose of political coverage the networks ever broadcast. Eight convention days took up as much TV airtime as the nine-week general election campaign did on nightly newscasts.

Admittedly, the nationwide audiences for the conventions were smaller than those garnered by most prime-time fare—Ronald Reagan's Dallas was no rival for J.R. Ewing's "Dallas"—but these smaller audiences packed a political punch. Three-quarters of registered voters told pollsters they watched the conventions on television at least one night, and from one-fifth to one-third of the voters have said they make their candidate choices during the late summer convention periods.

One last reason for assessing convention coverage: Network news directors have complained that media analysts confine their research to the few seconds that appear on the nightly news and ignore "what we do when we have more time." With two to four hours airing each night, conventions provide an excellent opportunity to examine how network reporters conveyed key battles of American politics in 1984.

Convention Speeches

Timothy Klein, Tonya Smith, Leslie Suelter, and I analyzed 39½ hours of CBS News and NBC News convention videotapes from the Vanderbilt TV News Archives—typical Central Standard Time zone versions of the conventions, with few interruptions for local news. (Limited resources prevented us from looking at all networks.) CBS News and NBC News allocated close to 40 percent of their airtime at each convention to speeches from the podium. Both networks gave the Democrats over two hours more coverage than the Republicans received, including an extra hour of Democratic oratory.

Although most convention coverage consisted of reporters and anchormen talking to one another and conducting interviews, it did offer a rare chance to hear several hours of extended, largely unedited, political speeches—far more than any other time on ABC News,

Table 1

VOTING RECORDS OF HOUSE AND SENATE REPUBLICANS AND DEMOCRATS VS. CBS NEWS AND NBC NEWS 1984 CONVENTION INTERVIEWS

All Congressional Democrats	TV's Convention Democrats	All Congressional Republicans	TV's Convention Republicans
CONSERVATIVE 8%	15% Coelho Coelho Hollings		70% Helms Cheney Denton Goldwater Goldwater Goldwater Dole Dole Dole Laxalt Laxalt Wilson Gingrich Lott Kemp Kemp Kemp Baker
MODERATE 36%	85% Melcher Melcher Glenn Mineta Lautenberg Ferraro Ferraro Wirth Wirth Wirth Hart Harkin Pepper Leland	CONSERVATIVE 62%	
LIBERAL 56%			
		MODERATE 31%	Weber Kassebaum Percy Snowe
	O'Neill O'Neill O'Neill O'Neill	LIBERAL 7%	Leach Leach Weicker Weicker

CBS News, or NBC News. (Usually only C-SPAN viewers have this chance.)

During these periods when network journalists were not talking, the major prime-time speakers naturally reflected the dominant elements of each party. Those given more than ten minutes of airtime from San Francisco were liberals: Mario Cuomo, Tip O'Neill, Jesse Jackson, Gary Hart, George McGovern, Jimmy Carter, Geraldine Ferraro, Edward Kennedy, and Walter Mondale. Those with over ten minutes from Dallas were conservatives: Jeane Kirkpatrick, Katherine Ortega, Jack Kemp, Gerald Ford, Barry Goldwater, Paul Laxalt, George Bush, and Ronald Reagan.

But the cameras used less than half their time relaying speeches from the dominant groups in each party, and the remaining hours may have been at least as important. In those hours of interviews, interpretations, and commentary, how did the networks depict the American political configuration? What issues did they elevate as most relevant to the electorate?

Democratic Disunity

The story the networks could have told has developed over the last 100 years. In that time, only one northern Democrat has received a majority of the popular vote for president—Franklin D. Roosevelt. All other Democratic presidents either won with pluralities or came from the South.

SHOE   JEFF MacNELLY

SENATOR, SOME PEOPLE ARE SAYING THAT YOU ARE THE MOST INCOMPETENT, INEFFECTIVE GUY IN THE WHOLE SENATE....

WHAT?!

WHO'S BEEN SAYING THAT?

WELL, THERE'S ME.... AND THE BOYS AT THE PRESS CLUB BAR.

Reprinted by permission: Tribune Media Services

In four of the last five presidential elections, the Democrats' share of the vote failed to exceed 43 percent: Hubert Humphrey received 43 percent in 1968; George McGovern, 38 percent in 1972; Jimmy Carter, 41 percent in 1980; and Walter Mondale, 41 percent in 1984. Georgian Jimmy Carter's narrow 1976 majority was the sole exception.

Volumes have been written about the collapse of the New Deal coalition, and they have made at least this much elementary: Along with many blue-collar workers and southerners, a wide range of people who think of themselves as Democrats, and who usually do vote for Democratic gubernatorial and congressional candidates, absolutely refuse to support undiluted, industrial-strength liberals for president.

As a result, a large share of all Democrats bolt their party and vote against liberal nominees: Over 30 percent of all Democrats voted against Humphrey in 1968; 33 percent voted against McGovern in 1972; 18 percent voted against Carter in 1976; 31 percent against Carter in 1980; and 24 percent against Mondale in 1984. With defections of this magnitude, there is no election contest.

This Democratic disaster is compounded by the Republicans' cohesiveness. Typically, only a small fraction of Republicans defect to vote for a Democrat for president. In 1984, for example, most exit polls found that fewer than 7 percent of the Republicans voted for Mondale.

That Democrats secured less than 45 percent of the vote in six of the past nine presidential elections is more than bad luck. The northern liberal Democratic candidates' failure to muster the support of less liberal rank-and-file Democrats is surely the fundamental dilemma for the party.

This may be either a sad situation, or the salvation of the Republic, depending on one's point of view, but the Democrats' divisions are no secret. How did CBS News and NBC News, each with nearly a dozen hours from the Democratic national convention, treat this historic drama?

Missing Interviews

CBS News and NBC News produced coverage that emphasized the crucial matter of Democratic party unity, but treated it as primarily dependent upon harmony among Walter Mondale, Jesse Jackson, and Gary Hart. The two networks rarely talked to moderate or conservative Democrats.

Table 1 contrasts the voting records of the senators and representatives who were interviewed by NBC News and CBS News with the overall congressional voting records of each party. The index used is a composite of the *National Journal* scores for liberal-versus-conservative voting on foreign, economic, and social policy.

As do most rankings, these show that over one-third of the Democrats in Congress vote in relatively moderate fashion, while nearly one in ten vote as conservatives. This substantial minority of nonliberals (43 percent) was dismissed by the networks that covered the Democratic convention. They interviewed *no* conservative congressional Democrats and only two moderates—Tony Coelho (twice) and Fritz Hollings, both liberal moderates. While liberals constituted 56 percent of all congressional Democrats, they received 85 percent of all the convention interviews conducted with senators and representatives.

A review of the noncongressional interviews reinforces this finding. We asked leaders of the Coalition for a Democratic Majority (CDM), a group of "Scoop Jackson Democrats," whether they recognized any like-minded friends among the fifty-two noncongressional interviewees; they spotted only one—Governor Charles Robb of Virginia.

Another two governors who were interviewed also have nonliberal reputations—Richard Lamm of Colorado and Joe Frank Harris of Georgia. Altogether, these three governors represent 6 percent of the noncongressional interviews. Most were with liberal delegates and people like Betty Friedan, Andrew Young, Patsy Mink, Joan Mondale, Harold Washington, and John Zaccaro.

When NBC's Chris Wallace interviewed Governor Robb, he asked: "As a moderate, do you feel 'odd man out'?" If he did feel out of place, it shouldn't have been with his party; in a 1982 CBS News/*New York Times* poll, a remarkable 76 percent of the Democratic rank-and-file said that they thought of themselves as moderates or conservatives, and the Democrats have a good number of moderates on Capitol Hill and in the statehouses. According to voting ratings, their Senate ranks include names like Chiles, Boren, Bentsen, DeConcini, Dixon, Exon, Ford, Heflin, and Johnston.

Moderate conservatives were by no means abundant on the floor of the Moscone Center, but under the circumstances, they might have been worth seeking. As it was, CBS News and NBC News treated moderate and conservative Democrats as less newsworthy than San Francisco's favorite transvestite, Sister Boom-Boom, and his Order of Perpetual Indulgence.

Missing Questions

The Democrats who are most likely to rebel against their party's current incarnation of liberalism—and those who are most likely to let a strong economy pull them into the Republican presidential column—are overwhelmingly those whose issue inclinations and self-identification are conservative-to-moderate. One might expect that this continued spectacular revolt against liberal leaders would prompt network inquiries about the rebels and why they again seem unattracted to their party's product. Instead, network discussions of party unity revolved around whether various liberal (although the word "liberal" was rarely used) factions would work hard for Mondale: would Jesse Jackson rally his troops for Mondale? Would Gary Hart stump for Mondale?

Would feminists energize the Democratic campaign?

Questions that explicitly pointed to the Democrats' ideological split were almost nonexistent, though there were a few notable exceptions. NBC's Ken Bode, for example, asked Tip O'Neill:

What do you tell those county chairmen in Texas who say, "We've got two Yankee liberals on the ticket, and we need to carry the state of Texas?"

And Dan Rather once asked O'Neill if he was worried "about putting two liberals at the top of the ticket." O'Neill assured him that there was no cause for concern. The networks, then, were not alone in overlooking the 39 percent of the rank-and-file who were unwilling to support Mondale.

Both CBS News and NBC News noted that convention participants were more liberal than the grass roots of the Democratic party, but they left the observation largely unexplained. John Chancellor did offer a few brief insights, explaining that there were "two Democratic tribes," and that the "activist liberals" in the hall wanted the platform to appear moderate so that it would appeal to "those of you who are Democrats at home, who are more moderate than these Democrats" at the convention.

Most unity discussions returned to Mondale's camaraderie with Jesse Jackson and Gary Hart. By the final night, network pundits pronounced the party united!

Missing Analysis

After Dallas, some annoyed Republicans claimed that networks kept their cameras on liberals Lowell Weicker and Jim Leach, but the critics were wrong. CBS News and NBC News may have dismissed Democratic conservatives, but they did not neglect Republican conservatives; Weicker and Leach did not dominate the screen.

As shown in table 1, conservative congressional Republicans were slightly overrepresented in TV interviews. Conservatives constituted 62 percent of the Republicans in Congress, but obtained 70 percent of the convention interviews. Liberal Republicans garnered two more and moderate Republicans four fewer interviews than proportionality would have indicated, although the moderate and liberal shares were bolstered by noncongressional interviews.

Overall convention exposure—on and off of the dais—was dominated by the prevailing conservative voices in the Republican party. Inattention was definitely not the problem for conservative Republicans that it was for moderate-to-conservative Democrats.

Another large difference in coverage of the two conventions was that the ideological dispositions of the Republicans were frequently noticed, classified, and commented upon, while such ideological analyses of Democrats at their convention were rare. On the average of about once every six minutes from Dallas, viewers were told that the Republican party was in the hands

of "very strong conservatives" or "the right wing" or "the hard right," with enormous power exercised by, in Walter Cronkite's words, the "fundamentalist religious conservative right wing."

San Francisco offered a sharp contrast. On the average of about once every hour, viewers heard Democrats mentioned as "a fairly liberal crowd" (Rather) who upheld "standard, liberal Democratic values" (Cronkite).

Several times, both CBS News and NBC News portrayed the Mondale-Ferraro approach as a move to the moderate middle: Dan Rather said Mondale wanted the party back in "the middle of the road," and he described the Democratic party's aim for a "centrist approach" and "a rush to the middle." He also called Ferraro's speech "pretty conservative."

Together, both CBS News and NBC News called the Republican party, its platform, or its dominant leaders by conservative labels 113 times. They called the Democrats by liberal labels 21 times and moderate labels 14 times.

No statistical summary can quite capture the verbal disparity in ideological labeling. To get a better picture, tables 2 and 3 list the ideological tags used by CBS News personnel to refer to party policies, groups, and all participants on the second nights of each party's convention.

Republicans were measured in ideological terms, with their distance to the right discussed and calibrated. Democrats were seldom evaluated by such criteria. The terms "right wing" and "right winger" appeared repeatedly in covering Republicans; the terms "left wing" and "left winger" were never used by CBS News or NBC News reporters covering Democrats.

Ironically, it was the liberal political tradition of Walter Mondale that was suffering. Even as reporters would not speak its name, most congressional Demo-

Table 2
CBS'S USE OF IDEOLOGICAL LABELS:
1984 DEMOCRATIC CONVENTION (SECOND NIGHT)

Phrase:	Reference:	Speaker:
"relatively conservative district"	Ferraro's district	Morton Dean
"a very, very conservative district"	Ferraro's district	Morton Dean
"the Archie Bunker district . . . his conservative philosophy resides there"	Ferraro's district	Morton Dean
"so-called moderate black politicians"	Black leaders not supporting Jackson	Ed Bradley
"left of the Democratic Party . . . he's to the left"	Jesse Jackson	Bill Moyers
"Tip O'Neill of Queens"	Geraldine Ferraro	Dan Rather
"a leftist politician"	Jesse Jackson	Bill Moyers
"a very liberal voting record . . . one of the most liberal congresspersons"	Geraldine Ferraro	Morton Dean

crats were busy running away from it and from Mondale/Ferraro. The alienation of a large chunk of the Democratic party continued to ensure defeat. Commentators' references to Democratic flag waving and endorsements of the family never explained why the party needed to invoke those symbols. By failing to dissect the Democrats' desertions and their ideological distance from the rank-and-file, the networks missed one of the critical stories of 1984.

Missing Issues

Partisans could emphasize their preferred issues when

Table 3

CBS'S USE OF IDEOLOGICAL LABELS:
1984 REPUBLICAN CONVENTION (SECOND NIGHT)

Phrase:	Reference:	Speaker:	Phrase:	Reference:	Speaker:
"ultraconservative platform"	Platform	Dan Rather	"interested in the fiscal . . . side of conservatism"	Pierre DuPont	Lesley Stahl
"too far to the right?"	Convention	Lesley Stahl	"two conservative wings"	Republican party	Lesley Stahl
"very strong conservatives"	Platform supporters	Diane Sawyer	"conservative wing"	Bush opponents	Dan Rather
"considered narrow ideologically"	Platform	Dan Rather	"social conservatives"	Republican majority	Bruce Morton
"the right wing"	Platform supporters	Bill Moyers	"conservative hit group"	NCPAC	Bill Moyers
"the fringe, the exotic radicals"	Terry Dolan and co.	Bill Moyers	"party of conservatives"	Republican party	Dan Rather
"aim is an authoritarian Republican party of moral absolutes"	New Right	Bill Moyers	"traditional conservatives"	Goldwater and others	Bill Moyers
			"Three main factions . . . two of them conservative"	Republican elements	Dan Rather
"party of far right conservatives"	Republican right	Bill Moyers	"other conservatives"	Ford and others	Dan Rather
"the hard right"	Republican right	Dan Rather	"traditional conservatives"	Ford and others	Dan Rather
"the hard right"	New GOP leaders	Dan Rather	"conservatives, more conservatives, liberal, moderate"	Republican party	Dan Rather
"billionaire . . . right-winger"	Bunker Hunt	Bill Moyers	"other conservative traditional wing"	Some Republicans	Walter Cronkite
"hard right conservatives"	Platform writers	Dan Rather	"economic conservatives"	Some Republicans	Walter Cronkite
"very conservative"	Platform	Bob Schieffer	"two right wings"	Republican party	Dan Rather
"too far to the right?"	Ronald Reagan	Dan Rather	"that endangered species, the Republican moderate"	GOP element	Dan Rather
"identify with the more conservative wing"	Jack Kemp	Dan Rather	"reaching out for the middle?"	Reagan's campaign	Bob Schieffer
"fundamentalist conservatives"	Republican element	Dan Rather	"center of the party is perhaps represented by . . ."	Pierre DuPont	Dan Rather
"fundamentalist, right-wing, conservative"	Platform writers	Walter Cronkite	"moderates"	GOP element	Dan Rather
"fundamentalist religious conservative right wing"	Republican element	Walter Cronkite	"moderates"	Non-Reaganites	Dan Rather
"religious fundamental conservative group"	TV preachers and conservative wing	Walter Cronkite	"told the moderates in this party, 'get out' "	By Terry Dolan	Dan Rather
maybe "Bush would be more conservative than Reagan . . ."	George Bush	Walter Cronkite	Republican "mainstream is a dry creek"	Jim Leach, etc.	Bruce Morton
"fundamentalist right"	Republican element	Dan Rather	"the moderates have no heirs"	Jim Leach, etc.	Bruce Morton
"populist . . . conservative . . . economic supply-sider"	Jack Kemp	Dan Rather	"liberal-moderate"	Ripon Society	Diane Sawyer
"several clicks more to the right than ever"	Platform	Dan Rather	"Republican liberal"	GOP element	Dan Rather
"pragmatic conservatives"	Those disturbed by platform	Dan Rather	"represents some of the more liberal members of his party"	Jim Leach	Dan Rather
"on the Republican right"	Vin Weber	Bob Schieffer	"liberals here are toothless, wingless, and hopeless"	GOP liberals	Bill Moyers
"conservatives would be proud of"	Platform	Bob Schieffer	"liberals"	Republican element	Dan Rather

22

they made their podium speeches, and such speeches took up 40 percent of all convention airtime. We distilled nine major themes from each convention's major addresses and acceptance speeches.

During most of prime time, reporters had independent opportunities to select the issues they deemed worthy of attention. They and their producers decided not only whom to interview, but also which issues to highlight. We coded every question asked by a CBS News or NBC News reporter according to subject.

In light of massive Democratic defections, one would have thought newsworthy questions would include those issues with which Republicans were apparently making headway: the growing economy, the decline of inflation, the Grenada intervention, and school prayer.

Instead, questions at both conventions came overwhelmingly from the Democratic agenda. As shown in table 4, policy-related questions drew on the Democrats' issues by a margin of at least seven to one. Consequently, Republicans were hit repeatedly with questions about matters the Democrats had stressed (especially arms control and E.R.A.), but Democrats rarely had to respond to the Republicans' issues.

This asymmetry meant that Democrats were almost never confronted with the possibility that the large loss from their own ranks might have something to do with preferences for the policies and performance of the opposition. In fact, Republicans were treated as if theirs was the approach that was in trouble. Some correspondents' queries from Dallas:

Lesley Stahl: There was no mention of arms control in your speech. . . . Why is that?

Tom Brokaw: There's been practically nothing said about arms control or a nuclear freeze or the need for some kind of summit to end the madness of the nuclear arms race. . . .

Chris Wallace: Are you concerned that there needs to be more talk about arms control and negotiations with the Soviets?

Tom Brokaw: There's not been much discussion at this convention about arms control. . . .

It would seem to be good journalism to confront both parties with the strongest arguments of their opposition. Even those who approve the press practice of "attacking the front-runner" must concede one thing: Shielding the underdogs from the issues that help the front-runners results in underplaying, or missing, some of the most influential factors of the campaign. The classic example of this was the economy.

Networks' summer polls showed no issue coming close to the economy and inflation in the hierarchy of voter priorities. Large numbers of people gave the Reagan administration some credit when they concluded the country was better off economically than it was four years earlier.

What, then, did CBS News and NBC News reporters ask convention politicos about the first postwar economic boom to increase family income and reduce unemployment without fueling inflation? Nothing. Does healthy adversarial journalism require minimizing topics that are inconvenient for the underdogs?

On to 1988

In nearly forty hours of convention coverage, CBS News and NBC News barely noticed two of the most powerful campaign factors of 1984: another epic defection of nonliberals from the Democratic ticket and the successful Republican appeals, most notably the booming economy. Ultimately, the summer polls correctly forecast that both factors would destroy Mondale's hopes.

On the road to 1988, it will be interesting to follow coverage of Democratic efforts to reassess party policies and strategies. The full spectrum of voices in the Democratic party seems to have been less easily heard than in the Republican party. How much attention will be conferred on the Bruce Babbitts, Mark Whites, and Chuck Robbs of the party? How much status will be accorded to the heirs of Henry Jackson? CBS News and NBC News may not have had much 1984 convention time to ask about the ideological quandary of the Democrats or the economic boom, but they did find time to include over forty questions about the 1988 presidential race.

Table 4
PARTY ISSUES AND NETWORK QUESTIONS
(Network totals combined from both conventions)

Republican Issues:	Questions: CBS News	NBC News	Democratic Issues:	Questions: CBS News	NBC News
Democrats too liberal	3	3	Republicans too conservative	7	11
Soviet military threat & need for a strong defense	2	3	Need to negotiate with Soviets & need for arms control	6	9
Lessons of Iran and Afghanistan	0	0	Danger of war in Central America	6	0
Success in Grenada	0	0	Failure in Lebanon	0	1
Economic boom	0	0	Federal deficit	5	3
Inflation down	0	0	Fairness issue	5	5
Opportunity society	0	0	ERA and women's rights	13	14
School prayer	0	0	Support social welfare & moderate defense spending	0	0
Deregulation	0	0	Environment & EPA	0	0
TOTAL	5	6	TOTAL	42	42

PART TWO

Media Coverage of the General Election

by Maura Clancey and Michael J. Robinson

General Election Coverage: Part I

Nineteen eighty-four's election victory may prove to be sweeter for conservatives than the election of 1980, and not so much because Reagan carried five more states or 8 percent more votes. In 1984, conservatives think they have what they lacked after the 1980 landslide—evidence that the television networks were guilty of liberal bias in covering the campaign.

In 1980 our research indicated that the networks covered "the issues" objectively and actually treated liberals worse than conservatives.[1] The networks covered liberal darling Teddy Kennedy more harshly than middle-of-the-roader Jimmy Carter during the early stages of that race, and then turned right around and treated Carter more negatively than Ronald Reagan during the rest of the campaign. In the end, the Carter-Reagan election news coverage was a mystery to those conservative press critics determined to unearth a "liberal" media.

But, at least at first blush, there seems to be little mystery this time: Right-of-center press watchers like John McLaughlin, Phil Nicolaides, and Pat Buchanan have already concluded, publicly and emphatically, that media coverage of Reagan, Bush, Mondale, and Ferraro supports their case concerning ideological bias in network news.

We don't know—can't know, really—if McLaughlin, Nicolaides, or Buchanan are correct about network motives. But our quantitative evidence from all three networks indicates that correspondents in the general election campaign of 1984 did, in almost every respect, treat Reagan and Bush much more negatively than Mondale and Ferraro.

In this two-part series, we plan to do three things with our data from 1984. In part one, we will document that Reagan and Bush received much worse press on network news than the opponents they defeated so handily. In this article, we'll also take on a second more difficult assignment. We'll argue that conservative critics are mostly *wrong* about the reasons the networks wound up carping more about the Republican than Democratic ticket and are wrong in believing that our data prove liberal bias in TV news.

In part two we'll consider what is the bigger story and clearly this year's greatest media mystery: how it was that Reagan and Bush could sustain so much more bad press than Mondale and Ferraro and still carry forty-nine states.

What We Did

Starting on Labor Day and continuing through election day, a team of five sifted through tapes from all three network evening news programs, distilling from about 200 broadcasts all the news about President Reagan or his White House; about the presidential or vice-presidential race; about lower level elections or state and local referendums. All told, we analyzed 790 stories, but for this report we concentrated on the 625 news items that dealt specifically with the presidential or vice-presidential campaign.

Every piece was scored on two dozen separate dimensions, some as straightforward as length or date of the story, some as slippery as press "spin" or ideological tilt. There is no magic to what we did—our training was collective, we used specific rules, and we reached consensus on almost every decision, despite the very different political views of our group.[2]

Reagan's "Packaging" vs. Mondale's "Coordination"

In mid-October, Roger Mudd did a report on this year's "spin patrols"—campaign officials or other partisans who flew to the debates and tried to put the best possible "spin" on their man's (or woman's) performance.

We were pleased that Mudd popularized the term "spin"; we had been using it as a variable since September. But to us spin means something different—the way the correspondent interprets or embellishes the facts in a story. Spin involves *tone*, the part of the reporting that extends *beyond* hard news. On October 12, for example, Ronald Reagan's train trip through western Ohio was hard news. But when Dan Rather chose to label the ride "a photo-opportunity train trip, chock full of symbolism and trading on Harry Truman's old turf," Rather added "spin."

Throughout, we scored every story for its spin—the positive or negative implications about the candidates contained within the reporter's own words. And we used "spin" as our first and most important test of good and bad press.

There are two important things to remember about the spin measure: First, when the reporter's subjective comments about objective facts went in both directions (positive *and* negative), we almost always judged the piece "ambiguous." Second, we *excluded* from our spin variable all references to the horse race, defining the spin as interpretations of the candidate's *quality*, not his *electability*.[3]

There may be some questions about the validity of our measure, but there can be no question about the lopsidedness of what it uncovered. Assuming that a piece with a positive spin equals "good press," and assuming that negative spin equals "bad press," Ronald Reagan and George Bush proved overwhelmingly to be the "bad press" ticket of 1984. Figure 1 contains the number of news seconds we scored as good press or bad press for each of the candidates.[4] Ronald Reagan's bad press total was *ten times greater* than his good

press total. (7,230 seconds vs. 730). In other words, his "spin ratio" was ten-to-one negative.

George Bush had a spin ratio that defied computation—1,500 seconds of "bad press" pieces and zero seconds of good press.

Walter Mondale and Geraldine Ferraro, on the other hand, had slightly *positive* spin ratios—1,970 seconds of good press about themselves as people or potential leaders, and 1,450 seconds of bad press. Given what we know about the bad news bias of television, the fact that anyone, let alone any ticket, got more positive spin than negative is news indeed.

These numbers don't, however, tell us everything about spin. When Edith Efron examined news coverage of the 1968 (Humphrey-Nixon) campaign, she neglected to include news coverage that had no observable spin—or that had ambiguous spin.[5] Efron's omission was a serious one. In 1984, 74 percent of the total time on network evening news devoted to national candidates had no clear spin, negative or positive. What we analyze here is the 26 percent that did. In fact, one of the best reasons for not getting too excited about the positive ratio for Mondale/Ferraro is that 86 percent (!) of their news coverage had no clear spin. Even George Bush, the candidate with no good press, might take some comfort from knowing that 60 percent of his news time was neutral or ambiguous.

In this regard, Reagan is tied with Bush. Forty percent, precisely, of Ronald Reagan's press coverage on network television showed spin, but, as we've already seen, 90 percent of that was negative.

What did Reagan's bad press look like in qualitative terms? Commentaries, as expected, focused on his policy failures. John Chancellor, for example, blamed Reagan for the security lapses in Lebanon; George Will and John Chancellor both complained about Reagan's having injected religion into America's secular politics. Bob Simon at CBS did a powerful news analysis on the failures of Lebanon policy since Reagan first took charge, making it clear that many Americans felt the Marines in Lebanon had indeed died in vain.

In the noncommentary pieces, Reagan came in for a different kind of criticism—a near-constant barrage of closers or interpretive remarks implying that something wasn't right with Reagan. He was hiding behind his security squad, he was cut off from the public, or he was manipulating symbols, or he was feeble-minded, or too old, or wasting taxpayers' money, or he was saying dumb things.

ABC's Sam Donaldson helped set the standard for bad tone with this mid-September piece:

Mondale may demand deficit reduction specifics, and the president answers with one-liners. Mondale may warn of hard times ahead, and the president points to good times at hand. Mondale may issue a call to arms, and the president waves the American flag. If there are true issues in this cam-

Figure 1

GOOD PRESS - BAD PRESS FOR EACH CANDIDATE

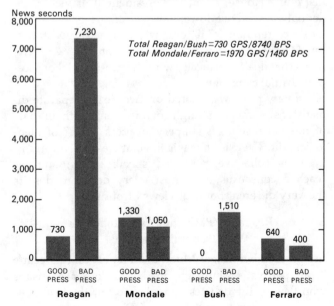

News seconds

Total Reagan/Bush = 730 GPS/8740 BPS
Total Mondale/Ferraro = 1970 GPS/1450 BPS

paign, they are being discussed but not joined.

And on October 4 Lesley Stahl did her quadrennial feature about the sinister nature of incumbency, focusing this time on Reagan's decision to run "a campaign in which he highlights the images and hides from the issues." Stahl told us that "the orchestration of television coverage absorbs the White House"; that "they aim to erase the negatives"; that "Mr. Reagan tries to counter the memory of an unpopular issue with a carefully chosen package (of videotape) that actually contradicts the president's policy." And Stahl even theorized about why Reagan "disappears" when things aren't quite right. "It's his gaffes," she concluded.

But NBC was at least as tough as CBS. (Table 1 suggests NBC was toughest across the board for all candidates.) And in fact, NBC did something that not only symbolizes Reagan's press problems, but also implies that Mondale did have (as our numbers indicate) an easier time of it on network news.

NBC's reporting is especially interesting because two very highly regarded correspondents essentially covered the same sort of action by Reagan and Mon-

dale, yet treated Reagan critically, Mondale almost sympathetically.

On October 16, Chris Wallace presented a long and captious piece about (what else) Reagan's Hollywood-style, made-for-TV news campaign. The Wallace piece lasted five minutes, it linked Reagan's campaign to the Nixon gang from 1972, and its message was clear—Reagan was all media and staging. In fact, NBC titled the piece, with logo, "Packaging Reagan."

Yet three weeks earlier, on September 27, Roger Mudd had presented a three-minute feature about Mondale/Ferraro media techniques and strategies. The Mudd piece was in no way flackery; Mudd even concluded that the Mondale "message" was not getting through. But Mudd treated the Mondale/Ferraro media machinations as a good thing. He spoke of a "coordinated message" and described the staff as "seasoned veterans." What had been "packaging" for Reagan was now "coordination" for Mondale.

Campaign Issues:
Nine of Ten Go against the Republicans

News has an agenda as well as a spin. Had the networks covered *only* Geraldine Ferraro's tax and financial matters during the campaign, regardless of the spin, that would have been a very different news agenda from one that included both her controversial tax returns *and* her adoring crowds. Had the networks covered only Reagan's record on inflation and never bothered to cover his record on deficits, that news agenda would have implied something important not just about Reagan but also about press behavior.

Of course, the networks did cover Ferraro's adoring crowds and did (though very infrequently) talk about Reagan's record on inflation. News agendas *are* tricky to define and even trickier to interpret, but in 1984 two interrelated findings about the news agenda suggest that the loser received better treatment than the winner on network news. The first has to do with what topics didn't get "normal" coverage in 1984. The second deals with the sort of topic that filled the vacuum.

(1) **Where's the horse-race news?** In virtually every campaign waged in the television era, the most frequent evening news story has been the on-the-road, horse-race piece—the reporter covers the day's campaign events and then assesses the candidate's motives and/or the electorate's possible response.[6] In 1984, though, horse-race journalism did *not* represent the most prevalent form of campaign reporting. *Campaign issues* pieces were emphasized instead. Campaign issues are not policy issues. Policy issues involve enduring disputes about how *government* should behave; campaign issues involve short-term concerns about how *candidates* or their campaigns should behave. In 1976, for example, a major campaign issue was Ford's remark about political freedom in Eastern Europe and what it indicated about his intelligence; in 1980 it was Carter's apparent meanness.

Table 1

PRESS SCORES OF JOURNALISTS (FOR ALL STORIES)

Journalist	Score
JOHN SEVERSON, NBC	−36
LISA MYERS, NBC	−30
PHIL JONES, CBS	−27
LESLEY STAHL, CBS	−25
BOB KUR, NBC	−22
CHRIS WALLACE, NBC	−21
RICHARD THRELKELD, ABC	−19
DEAN REYNOLDS, ABC	−14
GEORGE WILL, ABC	−12
SAM DONALDSON, ABC	−11
SUSAN SPENCER, CBS	−9
CAROLE SIMPSON, ABC	−9
CONNIE CHUNG, NBC	−7
JAMES WOOTEN, ABC	−6
ROGER MUDD, NBC	−3
PETER JENNINGS, ABC	−1
LYNN SHERR, ABC	0
BETSY AARON, ABC	0
KEN BODE, NBC	0
JOHN CHANCELLOR, NBC	0
DAN RATHER, CBS	+1
TOM BROKAW, NBC	+1
BRIT HUME, ABC	+2
BOB SCHIEFFER, CBS	+3
BARRY SERAFIN, ABC	+6
BRUCE MORTON, CBS	+6
TED KOPPEL, ABC	+7
RITA FLYNN, ABC	+8
BILL PLANTE, CBS	+18

Network	Score
NBC	−10
ABC	−4
CBS	−3

Note: These numbers represent the percentage of good press pieces minus the percentage of bad press pieces for each journalist and for each network for all candidate stories. The figures include "spin" on both dimensions, "personal quality" and "horse-race favorability." We include only those correspondents who presented at least seven stories about the campaign.

In 1984 campaign issues surged forward as a press focus, not only passing traditional horse-race reporting but also coming to represent almost *40 percent* of the campaign coverage.

There are two plausible explanations for the network's declining focus on the horse race and increasing interest in campaign issues. One, clearly, is that there was no horse race to cover. With Mondale/Ferraro consistently trailing in the polls, horse-race pieces became tiresome early on.

A second theory is that the media shifted to campaign issues when it became clear that emphasizing the horse race might be beneficial to the horse and jockey who were winning. If bandwagons still exist, horse-race journalism in 1984 could have been expected to help Reagan, and reporters could be expected to know it. Again, in these terms, Reagan and Bush came up short on the evening news.

(2) **The Agenda of Campaign Issues: Whatever Happened to John Zaccaro?** Horse-race journalism consumed less of the campaign news time in 1984, and what the networks used to fill the void made Reagan/Bush press losers again. In covering campaign issues, as opposed to policy issues, the news media are more free to pick and choose. This time, unlike 1980, they picked a news agenda that was decidedly bad for the Republicans.

Table 2 contains the twenty most fully covered "campaign issues" in the general campaign, debate coverage excepted. Nine of the top ten were campaign issues that were "bad news" issues for the GOP. Only one of the first ten was a bad news issue for the Democrats—the imbroglio between Geraldine Ferraro and her church, especially her verbal battle with Archbishop John O'Connor.

Reagan's suggestions that the Beirut embassy bombing was Carter's fault, or was akin to kitchen remodeling was the most fully covered campaign issue. The "age issue" came next: coverage of Reagan's having grown too old to debate, or maybe to think. Two nights after the debate ABC gave us three pieces in a row discussing Reagan's age: what we label the "senility trilogy." Next on the list was Reagan's "inaccessibility," one of the networks' favorites in September. Then Bush's feeble attempts to define "shame," from several dictionaries. Eventually the networks moved us on through the CIA manual controversy, the ties between Reagan and the fundamentalist preachers; the allegations concerning White House complicity in organizing hecklers against Mondale/Ferraro, and Bush's rudeness and personal behavior. The final of the top ten pieces was about "Donovangate."

Nothing says more about the network coverage in 1984 than this list of news topics. Neither Mondale's health problems (hypertension) nor Ferraro's confusion between "first use" and "first strike" made even the top twenty. Zaccaro/Ferrarogate comes in surprisingly low (Number 12). In toto, the Republicans endured a bad news agenda that was about five times greater than that given the Democrats (125 stories versus 25).

Table 2

AMOUNT OF ATTENTION GIVEN TO TOP TWENTY "CAMPAIGN ISSUES"*

1.	Beirut (as a campaign issue)	17 stories
2.	Reagan's age	15
3.	Bush's "shame" remark	12
4.	Reagan's availability	12
5.	CIA assassination manual	11
6.	*Ferraro vs. O'Connor/Church*	11
7.	Reagan/Religious ties	10
8.	Reagan/Heckler ties	9
9.	Bush's campaign behavior—("kick ass" included)	8
10.	"Donovangate"	8
11.	"Meesegate"	8
12.	*Ferraro/Zaccaro finances*	5
13.	Heckling/General**	5
14.	*Mondale/Gromyko meeting*	5
15.	Vetoes of journalists/debate one**	5
16.	Bush's blind trust/Taxes	4
17.	*Ferraro's credentials*	4
18.	Barbara Bush's remarks	3
19.	Campaign ethics generally**	3
20.	TV political ads**	3

Note: *Debate coverage is not included here. **Bipartisan issues. The issues in italics are those that focused on the Democrats.

Debate Coverage
Mondale 1, Reagan and Bush 0

The reality of the debates—who won, who lost—is as tricky a topic as any pundit can ponder. But nobody—not even Reagan—disputes that the president lost the first debate.

As for the second round, most print journalists felt that, given what he had to do, Reagan probably did win. And most polls showed that George Bush won the vice-presidential debate by either a little or a lot. The Democrats, then, won one debate by a lot, and the Republicans won two, but by much closer scores.

But this was not the picture we got from network news—at least not from the *personal* analyses presented by the on-camera correspondents. Looking at what the reporters concluded about the debates (when they were not merely reciting polls) one finds something remarkable: in twenty-seven stories, network correspondents made personal assessments implying either that Mondale had won the first debate or that Reagan had lost it. Not once did these reporters make any similar personal assessments about Bush's victory in his debate with Ferraro. And when Reagan won his second debate with Mondale, the network correspondents acknowledged it only twice, all the more remarkable given that Reagan's performance in the last debate probably mattered at least as much as his showing in the first. Indeed, Reagan received more than thirteen times as much evening news comment for losing the first debate as he did for winning his second.

On the day following the vice-presidential debate, the networks virtually ignored Bush's on-camera performance. All three turned instead to Bush's off-color, off-camera, off-handed remark about "kicking a little ass." Bush got more coverage for his "kick-ass" comment than for any other aspect of his debate appearance.

Horse-Race Predictions—
Finally: One for the GOP

Other than the good press Reagan got for his hurry-up meeting with Andrei Gromyko, did the networks favorably cover anything about him or his ticket? Yes, horse-race coverage was an unambiguous press victory for Reagan/Bush. Figure 2 contains the amount of

Figure 2

POSITIVE - NEGATIVE HORSE RACE FOR EACH CANDIDATE

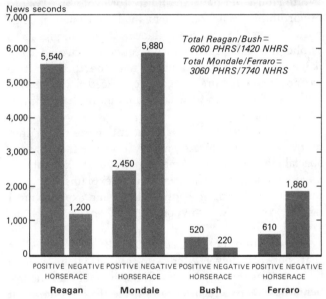

newstime for each ticket devoted to pieces in which the correspondent said or implied something favorable or unfavorable about the principal candidate's status in the horse race.

This measure tests whether the correspondent goes beyond citing polls and clearly implies that the campaign is going well or badly for the featured candidate. This is horse-race spin, in essence.

And spin about the horse race favored Reagan/Bush over Mondale/Ferraro. As figure 2 indicates, horse-race assessments ran four-to-one positive for Reagan/Bush three-to-one negative for Mondale/Ferraro.

Throughout the campaign, the Democrats complained more about press coverage than the Republicans. Democrats insisted that network correspondents were dumping on their man, their woman, and their campaign. The Democrats were right, but *only* when the "issue" was the horse race.

On the opening night of the general campaign, all three networks began what became a month's worth of

poor-mouthing the Democratic chances. NBC's Lisa Myers (see table 1) seemed particularly hard on Mondale's political condition, something the Mondale people noticed early on. Even after the first debate, the networks failed to give Mondale much copy suggesting he could somehow win the election. Mondale, in fact, earned much less credit for winning the first debate than Reagan was blamed for losing it.

On the other side, the networks did consistently give Reagan/Bush credit for winning the race and for conducting a "masterful" campaign. Even in those pieces we've already quoted about Reagan's packaging, Reagan's hiding out, or Reagan's cynical campaign strategy, the correspondents acknowledged that all his posturing was working. The news themes throughout suggested that Reagan was clearly winning, but, if the truth were known, he shouldn't be.

Cosmic Press Measure

Astute readers have already raised the crucial question. Was the bad press concerning Democratic chances in the race equivalent to the bad press concerning the personal qualities of the Republican ticket? We have no way of knowing how voters responded, but we do have a "cosmic" measure that combines the press spin about each candidate as a *person* with his or her press coverage of position in the race.[7]

The cosmic index, which tries to balance "horse-race" and "leadership" press coverage, is more than twice as negative for Reagan/Bush (—37) as for Mondale/Ferraro (—15). Bush got what everybody now expects—a cosmic score worse than everybody else's (—55), one that reflects constant references to Bush's poor judgment, his intemperate behavior, his political liability to himself and Reagan. Reagan came in second to last (—33). Ferraro finished with a —28, and Walter Mondale won a Pyrrhic press victory (—10). Even with the horse-race assessments factored in, the only definitive conclusion is that the networks gave Reagan/Bush a measurably tougher time than Mondale/Ferraro.

Denying Liberal Bias

Is it possible to prove that all this did not result from liberal bias in network news? In a word, no, but there may be a better explanation. Given that the networks covered the conservatives so much more negatively than the liberals, the only thing we can do is (1) assert that partisan bias is not the best explanation, and (2) come up with an alternate explanation. We believe we can justify doing both, though probably not to the satisfaction of many conservative critics.

The Whys

At this point, nobody appreciates more than we the now legendary Rothman-Lichter findings about liberal attitudes of the network news corps.[8] Though we have no data for 1984, it is inconceivable to us that Mondale/ Ferraro won less than the typical 85 percent of the vote "media elites" usually give to the Democrats in presidential elections.

But if it was "liberal" bias that the networks displayed in this general campaign, one has to ask some questions about the rest of the election year.

First, why did we find virtually no liberal bias on the policy *issues* in 1984? Of the 625 stories about the campaign, only 17 implied a liberal *or* conservative conclusion by the journalist on the issue at hand. And only 10 of the 17 were "liberal." What's more, most of those pieces were *commentaries*. The campaign *news* was practically devoid of issue bias.

Why did the liberal media never bother to mention Sonia Johnson or any of the other leftist candidates in the general campaign? And why did Mondale and Ferraro both wind up with negative cosmic scores?

And, we ask one last time, why in 1980, when the media had the chance to nip Reagan in the bud, did they give him less grief than they gave Carter? And why did they play it so negatively when Teddy Kennedy—a flesh and blood Kennedy—ran for president?

At the very least, these questions suggest that liberal bias is not the only explanation, or even the best.

Alternative Explanations

We know several journalists who are convinced that all this reflects nothing—or nothing but *reality*. To them news spin and news agenda were what the candidates deserved. In fact, we're even inclined to accept one of Reagan's own former White House people who invoked *reality* and said of George Bush: "He got bad press; he deserved bad press." But Bush is not Reagan, and Reagan's press is not simply reality.

We rejected the most sinister interpretation—that all or most of this press behavior reflects ideology. And now we also reject the most innocent interpretation— that Reagan's press involves nothing more than simple reality.

We refuse to believe, for starters, that reality explains why Reagan/Bush got five times as much news coverage of their problems (campaign issues) as Mondale/Ferraro, especially given all the allegations swirling around Ferraro.

Then what's left? We think the four "I's" have it: impishness; irritation; incumbency; and irrevocability. Taken together, with perhaps a dose of reality and a little touch of ideology as well, these four "I's" explain, we think, why Reagan/Bush looked so bad in the network news copy in this year's general campaign.

Impishness involves little more than Charlie Peters' old notion that reporters of all types prefer to cover a competitive horse race to a walkaway. So, journalists did little things to *produce* a horse race when none seemed to exist. Out of impishness, they played games with the news agenda, or even with spin, hoping to make the race tighten.

Some think impishness stems from commercial pressure—the need to maintain ratings. We think it's less commercial than personal—a human tendency to keep one's own work interesting—not so much for audiences but for those who themselves ride the news bus so long. Whatever the cause, judging by the tiny smirks on the correspondents' faces after the first debate, we think impishness explains at least some of the tendency to carp at Reagan/Bush more often than at Mondale/Ferraro.

But *irritation* strikes us as a bigger factor. Irritation suggests that network reporters behave less like leprechauns than prima donna professionals. Big-time campaign correspondents acknowledge that Reagan's skillful use of media time exasperated them. Since 1983, the press has consistently bemoaned what it considers Reagan's Teflon coating. But network people have an even further justification for feeling resentment—the White House *did* have an affinity for exploiting "photo opportunities" and one-liners in TV "cameo appearances." Given that Reagan's inaccessibility to press and public was the fourth most frequently covered campaign issue on network news, and the focus of two extraordinary features, we are convinced that irritation with the Teflon candidacy explains more than impishness in 1984.

But *incumbency* probably counts more than either of the above. Reporters simply feel that they have a special mission to warn Americans about the advantages any incumbent has. That, we believe, explains why Carter wound up doing so badly in 1980, and explains most of the content we saw on network news this time around.

Hal Bruno, political editor at ABC, acknowledges that network news winds up giving incumbents a tougher time. He says that reflects the fact that incumbents have active records to criticize. Fair enough. But we think it's both—a record to attack *and* a supposition by the media that the White House incumbent simply deserves a double standard from the press. It's the "compensatory journalism" that we saw in 1984. The press will always hold incumbents to a tougher standard, especially when they happen to be winning big in the race.

Irrevocability is a condition determined by the Twenty-second Amendment and its "two-term only" rule. Reagan would, if reelected, never face the electorate again. What more did the media need to justify a double standard in press coverage than Reagan's irrevocability in office? In short, the Constitution made them do it. When the press knows that this is the last shot voters will have—against a front-runner, no less— getting out the bad press becomes a near messianic mission.

Chris Wallace did something on election eve that proves the point. On election eve in 1980, all the network correspondents played it very straight when covering the candidate's last campaign day. It's the norm. After two long years of harassment, candidates can usually expect an election eve respite from bad press. But Wallace showed how seriously he was taking irrevocability when, in essence, he broke from that norm.

Wallace started out tough. "Today's sentimental journey through California ended the highly staged, low-risk campaign of a big front-runner." "A campaign long on glitz and short on substance, . . . a cynical campaign, manipulative." Wallace stayed tough: "Protecting a big lead, the president offered pomp and platitudes, but never told us what he planned to do the next four years." For Wallace, it was a last minute effort to get the bad news out before it was too late, with Reagan likely to go scot free in the morning.

None of this reporting, in retrospect, seems to have been inaccurate, let alone irresponsible. And quite clearly, the networks were not hyping Mondale/Ferraro in this campaign. What is clear is that with all the "I's" out against him, Reagan could have expected that the media would engage in a little naysaying about his campaign. Reagan was the incumbent, was ahead, was good at exploiting official symbols, and was saddled with a less capable running mate. What's more, Reagan really was and is a conservative candidate, a fact that could not possibly have helped him in the national press.

Given all of this, it was predictable that all the networks would practice a little compensatory journalism. Compensatory journalism shouldn't surprise—or even infuriate—anybody who understands the press. What did surprise a good number of pundits is how little difference any of this compensatory journalism seems to have made. And that surprise—the lack of

impact—requires a second look. Next time we will look at what the networks did *not* do in 1984, and try to explain why voters paid so little heed to the news agenda and news spin that the networks were handing out in this campaign.   ☑

1 *Over the Wire and On TV: CBS and UPI in Campaign '80*, Michael Robinson and Margaret Sheehan, Russell Sage Foundation, 1983.

2 In the article we provide our definitions as we go along, section by section. But one important qualification needs to be made at the outset. We analyzed the journalists, their copy, and their nonverbal gestures. We did *not* analyze the candidates or their surrogates. If Reagan smiled warmly on camera or told an hilarious joke, we excluded Reagan's performance from our assessment of *news* content. We scored not what Reagan said or did, but instead what Sam Donaldson, Chris Wallace, or Bill Plante *et al.* said or did. Our entire emphasis here is on journalism, not the comprehensive "message." And it was the *journalism* that went very much against Reagan, warm smile or one-liners notwithstanding.

3 Obviously we realize that reporters also employ "spin" in discussing the horse race. And we have a separate measure that allowed us to keep track of the way the networks treated each candidate's *chances*. But in 1980 we learned that network reporters tend to divide their news interpretations into two categories—those related to personal quality and those related to candidate status in the race. So we did the same in 1984: For us "spin" involved the reporter's remarks concerning the candidate's credibility, availability, vitality, integrity, consistency, decency, or "factuality." In essence, spin includes everything *but* "viability."

4 We scored this for the *principal* candidate only. If a piece dealt with two candidates equally, we divided the story, and the time, in two.

5 *The News Twisters*. Edith Efron, Nash Publishing, 1971.

6 *The Unseeing Eye: The Myth of Television Power in National Elections*, Thomas Patterson and Robert McClure, G.P. Putnam, 1976; *The Mass Media Election: How Americans Choose Their President*, Thomas Patterson, Praeger, 1980.

7 Cosmic measures for each candidate also include scores for news *topics*. A piece about Ferraro's fight with her church gives her a negative *one*, and if the "spin" is negative also, then Ferraro gets a minus two for the piece.

8 S. Robert Lichter and Stanley Rothman, "Media and Business Elites," *Public Opinion*, October/November 1981.

The authors appreciate the support given this project by the George Washington University and by AEI. We also thank Lisa Grand, Eve Raimon, Maryann Wynne, Carin Dessauer, and Bobbie Chilcote for helping us do this research.

by Michael J. Robinson

The Media in Campaign '84: Part II Wingless, Toothless, and Hopeless

Reagan's age, Reagan's gaffes, Reagan's ties to the extreme right, Reagan's running mate. By the end of Campaign '84, these network evening news stories were as familiar as motels in Breezewood, Pa. But in the end these stories didn't matter. The networks never managed to tarnish Reagan's image or diminish his lead. Why was that?

In our last article, Maura Clancey and I looked at one aspect of network news performance during last year's campaign: how the candidates were covered. Our conclusion was that Reagan/Bush lost out to Mondale/Ferraro in terms of news spin and news agenda: The networks had nipped harder at the Republicans than the Democrats in every respect except evaluation of the horse race. (*Public Opinion*, December/January 1985)

The focus of this article, Part II of our campaign coverage evaluation, is different. Instead of documenting the network coverage of the candidates per se, this second look explains why the networks seemed so ineffectual, and asks whether their ineffectuality was unique to 1984 and the Reagan presidency. It *is* possible that the media coverage of the 1984 general election says more about the networks and the news media than it does about Ronald Reagan and his special relationship with the American people.

Press and Opinion: A Hollywood-Style Relationship

The aggregate statistics imply that the network newspeople had practically no meaningful impact on the electorate, especially if one looks only at the spin variable—innuendo and comment about each candidate's leadership qualities (what most people think of when they think of "bias"). During the general campaign, as we measured spin, Bush fared worst (−40); Reagan was third (−33); Mondale eked out a +1; and Ferraro had the most positive spin—a total of +4.[1]

Few could deny, however, that Reagan wound up more favorably regarded than Mondale. The same holds true for Bush: throughout the campaign, Bush maintained higher favorability ratings than his opponent did despite Bush's dismal press spin score—the worst of all candidates. (Ferraro's was the best—at least in September and October.) So, the major determinant of public opinion clearly was something other than network spin.

These aggregate measurements may, however, conceal something. What happens when we look not at the big picture, but at weekly snapshots of network spin, correlated with measures of each candidate's public image? Using Patrick Caddell's "thermometer score" (a gauge of the public's attitude toward the quality of the candidate) and our own spin measure, we found that the relationship over time was almost as weak as the aggregate measures had implied.

For Ferraro, the correlation between spin and image was actually negative (−.33), which means when Ferraro's press was bad, her image was good and vice versa. That correlation probably does not mean that the public rejected the network news line on Ferraro, but may mean that, by October, the networks decided Ferraro was so far behind there was no point in doing any more negative spinning about her. Ferraro was, after all, at best a losing vice-presidential nominee. The *negative* correlation 'twixt Ferraro's press and Ferraro's image suggests, in fact, that in some circumstances the polls influence the news media more than the other way around. Neither Bush nor Mondale seemed to suffer (nor to benefit) much from their week-to-week press spin;[2] the correlation between their spin and image was statistically insignificant. For Mondale, the figure was −.07; for Bush +.18.

Only Reagan seemed to show any positive relationship between his spin measure and the Caddell thermometer score: When his press got worse, so did his favorability rating, at least slightly. But for Reagan, too, the statistical tie between spin and image was negligible

(+.32). Even so, that figure provides one of the most intriguing results in our research: the supposedly impervious candidate was the only one of the four who tended to lose support when his press got bad.

In truth, the relationship between Reagan's press image and his popular image had as much to do with statistical vaguenesses as with media impact. If one looks with one's eyes, instead of one's computer, at Reagan's press scores and his favorability scores during the general campaign, one finds a final form of evidence to support the basic premise that the news media had little effect in the general campaign of 1984.

Table 1 contains our weekly reading of both press measures—Reagan's spin score (innuendos about his competence, availability, decency, consistency) and his viability score (references to his electability or standing in the race). Table 1 also contains a third line—the Caddell favorability measure as it was assessed, time after time, during the campaign.

There is some congruity here. On the week when Reagan had his best press score, he did his best at incurring favor with his public. And when his press was at its worst (after the first debate), his thermometer score was at its lowest. But Reagan's press measures jumped up and down as violently as March temperatures in Washington. His favorability scores, on the other hand, varied little more than year-round temperatures in Santa Barbara. And, of course, Reagan's favorability scores were always positive, while his press scores were mostly negative.

There *is* a relationship between these lines, but it isn't much sturdier than a two-star Hollywood marriage. So, for the Final Four 1984 candidates, the relationship between press and public opinion was weak. Having lost the war for spin and agenda on network evening news, the Republicans won most everything else. Having won the war for spin, the Democrats won Minnesota.

Truths about Network News

How is it possible that a nation that relies so heavily on network news for monitoring presidential elections could seem so impervious to news spin or even news agenda? Apart from the Democrats' explanation—that Reagan himself is the answer—let's concentrate on two other factors: what the networks *didn't* do or say in this election, and what the electorate generally fails to do in most elections.

Once one has set aside the innuendos about the candidates' behavior and motives, it becomes fairly clear that in 1984 the networks did not do nearly enough to overcome real events, real conditions, and real style. In short, the network coverage was so "responsible" that it carried almost no weight in the general campaign. What remains, then, is to document all the things the networks didn't do in this election that might have made them a real factor. We should also consider whether the networks *ever* behave in a way that could determine electoral preferences or outcomes.

Don'ts and Didn'ts

Qualitatively and quantitatively, the Republicans had a measurably tougher time on evening news in the general election, especially when one looks at candidate spin and campaign issues coverage. But when one looks beyond these topics, there is a long list of things the networks did not do in 1984.

We need to consider the long list.

(1) **No Bias by Time:** One theory in media research holds that time on camera is influence. The theory states unequivocally that media exposure inherently and inevitably produces support for the person exposed. My guess is that Joseph Mengele and Constantin Chernenko would deny that premise. (Neither was available for comment.) Still, one could argue that had the networks given disproportionate time to Mondale/Ferraro—to make their case or just to smile warmly—that might have moved voters in a Democratic direction. Walter Mondale now suggests that had the networks given him more screen time, he would have done worse politically.[3] But whatever the real impact of exposure, the networks did *not* in 1984 show bias by time.

The Republicans received approximately 25,000 seconds (21,178 for Reagan and 3,780 for Bush) of newtime in their *campaign* coverage; the Democrats received about 26,000 seconds (19,970 for Mondale and 6,390 for Ferraro). That works out to approximately six seconds more per program for the Democrats—less, actually, than our rounding procedure may have given either side by accident. When one adds time spent covering Reagan as president, there is no advantage for the Democrats, but, in fact, a Democratic time deficit.

Time is the crassest of content measures, but we also found that the networks practiced "fairness by quotation" throughout the campaign. In 1984 the networks quoted neither side or both sides in the majority of cases. In those few cases where one side was quoted exclusively, it tended to be the Republicans.

The networks gave practically no time to the minor parties, other than pieces about Bob Richards and his radical-right version of the new Populist Party of America. But in covering the major parties, the networks played it fairly and equally. The granting of equal time to both sides helps explain how it is that news spin doesn't necessarily matter much. In this case, Reagan and Bush had time to work around and through much of the innuendo.

(2) **No Issue Bias:** It's been more than thirty years since Joseph McCarthy labeled Edward R. Murrow and CBS News part of the "jackal pack" of Communist sympathizers. The rhetoric has cooled since then, but the struggle continues. Jesse Helms and his friends are mad, and they're trying to get even. Their plan is to buy up CBS News stock and put a stop to that network's "liberal bias." When he laments network liberal bias, Helms seems specifically to have in mind the 1984 campaign.

Interestingly enough, the public doesn't see much

partisan bias on network evening news.[4] Basically, the public is right, at least as far as our data about the issues are concerned. Even though spin and the campaign-issues agenda went against the Republicans in 1984, ideological bias about substantive matters hardly existed on evening news—not even on CBS.[5]

All told, our 1984 study included 826 news pieces.[6] Searching for issue bias, we went on a word-by-word search for any subjective statement by the reporter (or any "bias by quotation") that implied either a liberal or a conservative conclusion about the policy involved. But we found practically no issue bias on network evening news.

Only 2.5 percent of all the pieces implied a liberal position *or* a conservative position on any issue discussed in the piece. Part of that is because over half the news contains "no issue content" (fewer than two sentences). But that sorry truth ought not to obscure the more important, happier truth: only twenty-one pieces suggested a point of view on a policy issue. Eleven of those pieces implied a liberal point of view; ten seemed to us to be conservative. That represents a plus-one advantage for the liberals in a sample of 826 news reports, but this hardly constitutes a liberal victory. And it is hardly enough to move an electorate—even a liberal electorate. More important, the majority of those twenty-one pieces that showed bias were *commentaries*, the appropriate place for policy opinion. In the end, none of the networks displayed much ideology, and CBS News was as innocent as the rest.

Even when the networks appeared to be concentrating on campaign issues that might make the Republicans look bad, they kept subjectivity to a minimum. In covering campaign issues, there was bias by topic, but that rarely extended into the copy through subjective statements or innuendo. Excluding debate reports, we identified 140 full-fledged campaign issue pieces. The majority of them made the Republicans look bad, at least by topic (Reagan's age, Bush's rudeness). Yet in most cases, the networks neither blamed nor exonerated the candidate for any allegations presented in these campaign issue pieces.

There was some asymmetry in all this. When the networks conveyed a conclusion about the campaign issue at hand, the Republicans suffered from negative conclusions more than nine times out of ten. But in six cases out of seven, all the networks seemed content just to *raise* the issue, not to settle it by conveying guilt or innocence.

(3) **No Imperial Journalism:** In 1984, the networks lacked bite because they also failed to do those imperial and arrogant things they are presumed to do in every election. Consider first their use of verbs and adjectives.

Most political leaders remember every time the media used an insinuational verb against them: "he conceded," for example, instead of "he said." But in 1984, the networks used insinuational verbs rather sparingly. We made a list of insinuational verbs—verbs that implied something sinister about the speaker—and then poured through each piece looking for them. Our list was fairly restrictive (we did *not* consider a verb such as "insists," for example, to be so much insinuational as implicative) but our findings were still surprising: 91 percent of the campaign news items contained no insinuational verbs. The networks treated the Democrats and Republicans alike. Reagan and Bush were the objects of insinuational verbs in just under 10 percent of their campaign coverage; Mondale and Ferraro were about the same. But the more important finding here is that only 9 percent of the stories contained any loaded verbs at all.

The same holds true for adjectives. Using William Adams' research as a guide,[7] we had expected that the networks would be more likely to use pejorative adjectives to describe conservatives than to describe liberals. We were correct. We found eight times as many references to the "far right" as to the "far left." Network officials claim (note the verb) that that merely reflects the reality of 1984—there is no left wing in active presidential politics any more, while there is an active right wing. Perhaps. But the more interesting thing is that that ratio—eight to one—masks a more remarkable statistic. Only 18 stories out of more than 800 made any reference to *either* wing. In essence, adjective bias existed only at the margins. In the end, the networks were even more reluctant to practice subjectivity by adjective than by verb.

Then, too, we found the networks behaving almost passively when it came to establishing an issues agenda. Such was not the case with *campaign* issues. But when it came to substance issues, the networks followed the candidates' agenda, not their own. The most frequently

---

Table 1

WEEK-BY-WEEK "SPIN" AND "VIABILITY" SCORES FOR REAGAN
CADDELL THERMOMETER READINGS FOR REAGAN

	September				October				November
	1st week	2nd week	3rd week	4th week	1st week	2nd week	3rd week	4th week	1st week
Caddell thermometer			63	64	62 64	62	64	66	65
Reagan "spin"	−47	−16	−46	−22	−34	−57 −34	−26	+2	0
Reagan "viability"	25	34	21	17	24	−5 +9	23	60	38

Note: The author wishes to thank Patrick Caddell and Cambridge Survey Associates for making these data available.

addressed issues on TV were the most frequently addressed issues in reality: taxes, religion, U.S.-Soviet relations, deficits, and so on.

The networks gave tax issues the biggest play—two and a half times as much as deficits. If the networks had wanted to move votes toward Mondale in this election, that agenda would have been tailor-made for failure. But the networks followed the candidates' lead on issues in this campaign. And with the heavy news emphasis on tax issues, one can understand why Reagan did well on network news, even if the campaign-issues agenda was moving against him. All told, the issues agenda on evening news was a wash, reflecting what both candidates really were talking about.

We also checked the networks for subliminal bias via nonverbal communication. For us that meant meaningful voice inflection, eye gesture, body language, or video used to make an unstated point. To be fair to the networks and ourselves, we ignored nonverbal communication that simply reinforced the printed text. When ABC's Jim Wooten used a close-up of Reagan's very old-looking hands, for example, to make the point that Reagan is old, we did not classify the video as subliminal bias, since Wooten's whole piece was about Reagan's aging and the "age issue." The important point is that in over 90 percent of the news pieces, there was no meaningful nonverbal communication. Excluding pieces that contained a sarcastic voice inflexion (the least sinister of the nonverbal signals), the percentage of straight pieces—those without nonverbal cues—jumps to 98. The networks failed to cost Reagan any votes by what they said, and it is also fairly certain they cost him no votes by the way they said it. They simply did not practice nonverbal communication.

All of this implies an important reality about network news in 1984. They did use spin. They did build a campaign-issues agenda that looked suspicious. But they did not go off half-cocked or half-baked.

The best evidence probably involves evening news coverage of Reagan's age, a classic illustration of what networks will and won't do. Reagan's age eventually ranked as the number two campaign issue on evening news—the subject of fifteen separate pieces. (Only Reagan's remarks following the embassy bombing in Lebanon got more play.) But none of the networks touched the age issue until Reagan justified the coverage with his performance in the first debate. In fact, the networks held off even then, until the *Wall Street Journal* decided to make it a front-page story. The day the *Journal* made age a legitimate issue was the day the networks, especially ABC,[8] seized it for the first time.

So we come to an important conclusion: in 1984, despite some tougher press for the Republicans, the networks practiced fair and responsible journalism. They gave the GOP an equal chance to make its case; they gave the public a clear indication that the GOP was winning; and they gave Reagan opportunities to flash his smile and use his one-liners. Compared with news spin

and campaign-news agenda, these things would almost certainly permit the Republican ticket to carry the day and the Electoral College. And so it was. All that remains now are two bigger questions: First, was this coverage in 1984 exceptional or was it the rule? Second, was the voters' response (or lack of response) unique to Reagan and his Teflon coating or is this the way the electorate generally behaves?

Is 1984 Unique?

Rolling Stone's William Greider seems to believe that the networks were unusually craven in this campaign.[9] He singled out Roone Arledge as the accomplice in emasculating network campaign journalism, claiming that Arledge had sold out to the new patriotism in order to make Olympic coverage a better show, benefiting Reagan in the process.

Greider is, in my mind, wrong if he believes that 1984 campaign reporting was in any way exceptional. In 1980, Margaret Sheehan and I found the same patterns—near-total objectivity on the issues; news spin decidedly less positive about the incumbent (Carter) or the early frontrunners (Kennedy and Reagan); a campaign issues agenda that reflected the networks' definitions of journalism; a substance issue agenda that reflected what the candidates really wished to address.[10] The 1984 coverage duplicates 1980's almost exactly.

There was one major difference between the last two campaigns: there was no hostage crisis in 1984, even though there were American hostages being held in the Middle East during *both* campaigns. But in a bizarre way, the hostage crisis of 1980 and the hostage non-crisis of 1984 reinforce the basic premise—that networks usually act responsibly, if not passively, in most of the substantive aspects of campaign reporting.

Roone Arledge, Greider's villain in 1984, actually played a big part in the "America Held Hostage" syndrome in 1980, helping Reagan then, too. But Jimmy Carter played a much bigger role in making the hostage crisis a media crisis. Carter chose to publicize, dramatize, personalize, and sensationalize the hostage story, and eventually, like a sorcerer's apprentice, found himself unable to staunch the flow of hostage news he had helped bring forth. The networks followed Carter's leadership on the hostage story. Not surprisingly, Reagan's people chose precisely the opposite tack with the 1984 hostage problem, and the networks accepted it. With no "news," they dutifully ignored the American hostages held captive in Lebanon throughout the 1984 campaign.

In essence, then, network news behaves in the same way from year to year. *Leaders* behave differently, and that changes news practice. Networks follow the leaders in any campaign—acerbically, to be sure, but in such a way that any impact on opinion choice is the exception, not a binding rule.

Where the networks get uppity is on the campaign issues—those watchdog-style issues. And that too has been the rule. If the networks *have* teeth, it's on these campaign issues. But, of course, it's on these campaign issues that the networks usually dull their teeth and waste their time. Nobody ever cared about Watergate, at least not in 1972. Nor did Billygate matter to the public in 1980. It was the same with Meesegate—press concern was unmatched almost completely by public concern. [11] Networks, like all national news sources, exhaust themselves on the sorts of campaign issues that the electorate finds ho-hum, assuming it finds them at all.

Is Reagan Unique?

There is a word for those who consider only content when discussing media impact: stupid. I have forced the discussion toward content because, after all, content is what we studied in 1984. Obviously, voters count too. Yet conventional wisdom about the electorate may, in light of this campaign, prove as misconceived as the conventional wisdom about the news itself.

The first misconception—and the broadest—is that the American news audience has, in the age of television, turned against incumbents. House incumbents do marvelously in reelection bids; Senate incumbency has, since 1980, made a remarkable comeback. And the fact is, presidential incumbents have not done at all badly in gaining audience support for their reelection in this, the television age.

Since Hoover, only *one* duly elected presidential incumbent has been defeated for reelection: Jimmy Carter. Kennedy probably would have been reelected. Johnson might well have been. Richard Nixon was reelected, carrying 49 states. Incumbents who attempt it are far more likely to win reelection in the broadcast era (from 1932) than those in the pre-broadcast era. Given almost any reason to do so, the electorate generally prefers to reelect the devil it knows.

My own guess is that incumbents have always had a tougher press than challengers. So, in 1984 we did not have an historic election in terms of media content or in terms of electoral response. As usual, an incumbent got the short end of the media spin and the long end of the popular vote. Despite the news spin or agenda, incumbents can do all right, so long as they have something else going for them.

This leads us to Reagan, an incumbent who had lots going for him. Reagan was able to work through or around his press—virtually any incumbent can, as long as *conditions* are favorable. The fact is, no president needs good press. He needs only good news. We've already seen that Reagan lost support when his press turned awful, most vividly after the first debate. But news spin and news agenda have almost no major impact on an incumbent when the news itself is good. In a race that starts with a twenty-point gap, spin and campaign issues agendas won't come close to making it a contest. Even though the networks never hyped the recovery, they covered it. Even though the networks continued to spin negatively about Grenada during the

1984 election campaign (CBS's David Martin presented an anniversary piece about the "sanitized war" in Grenada which made our military conduct there look much less than heroic), the networks covered the students, the flags, and the polls.

As long as the media do not conspire to keep major events and conditions away from the audience—and they do not—their news agenda and news spin will have almost no impact when compared with real news. Win a little war; have the nation's long distance runners do well at the summer Olympics; sit there as employment returns to the level at which you took office; the electorate will beat a path to your door a second time. Think not? Ask Margaret Thatcher, the United Kingdom's "Teflon candidate," a woman who is to free media performance in the TV age what John Riggins is to dinner etiquette. Would anyone argue that two-term, "landslide" Richard Nixon was the Great Communicator or Teflon coated? The electorate will almost never pay serious attention to spin or campaign issues agenda if things are good. Newspeople recognize this: why shouldn't we?

Weak Data or Weak Media?

From the very beginning of this research, our critics have blasted us for our methodology—for not taking into account Reagan's "free media performance," how he handled *himself* during the news. And those who insist Reagan is *sui generis* score points when they argue that Reagan made his own good press by saying clever things, by smiling warmly, by orchestrating a superb campaign. Their argument is simple: without having factored in Reagan's free media performance, our research and unorthodox conclusions are based on weak data.

Fair enough. If Reagan could dispel the age issue with a one-liner in the last debate (the press said so), free media performance is important. If Reagan can crack a smile and a joke while Chris Wallace implies that Reagan is all show, who cares what Wallace says? I accept all that—especially the part about free media performance as an antidote to bad press. But my own assessment is that our methods and data are not weak—it is, instead, the *media* that are weak. Despite our initial finding that spin and agenda went against Reagan and Bush, this second set of findings shows something different: The networks practiced no ideological bias; granted candidates equal "time"; covered Reagan's lead and almost all his laugh-lines; and made subjective assessments about only trivial sorts of things like "motives." Our methodology shows what I now consider the larger truth—that spin and campaign news agenda are almost all the networks are willing to risk in a presidential campaign, and they are hardly freewheeling enough with those to move an electorate.

Given what we found in the overall coverage—what was *said*—network news power in a general election boils down to innuendo and to campaign issues.

Compared with real events, real conditions, and free media performance, those powers will usually prove to be minimal, at least once the nominations are secure.

The networks, outside of presenting hard news and fact, have far less influence on voters than most critics—and most campaign managers—assume. In 1984, the networks wound up weaker than our data. The fact is, the networks ought to embrace our findings—showing as they do that the networks used only a little innuendo: They did it justifiably, did it responsibly, and did it without much effect.

The Responsible Electorate

Nineteen eighty-four has produced a host of news media mistakes—not so much by the news media as *about* the news media. Fortunately for me, the mistakes run from left to right. The left is wrong in believing that the networks let Reagan go scot free. William Greider must have been watching a different election from the one we saw on network news.

The Democratic establishment has it wrong too. Reagan is *not* impervious to bad news. He even showed some vulnerability to bad press—more than his opponents, in fact, even if not all that much in the end.

Walter Mondale is off the mark as well. This was not an election decided on the basis of free media performance. Reagan was as effective on television in 1983 as in 1984, when two-thirds of the public disapproved his presidency and John Glenn was leading him in the trial heats by more than ten points. If John Glenn can lead you in the polls, you are not, by any stretch, a political Houdini. Ronald Reagan took the oath this January less popular than Truman was in January 1949, than Eisenhower was in January 1957, than Johnson was in January 1965. Why would anybody need to explain the magic on the basis of free media performance when the magic is almost commonplace? Take away Grenada, Mary Lou Retton, the end (almost) of inflation, the return of investment and jobs, and free media performance is a weak reed.

The network news people have their own blinders about 1984. They insist that our spin measure is ill-conceived (a real possibility) and that they covered only Reality. In a news world where Reagan's dirty tricks and ties to hecklers in California (all unproven to be sure) get nine times as much attention as Mondale's real health, this is not reality with a capital R.

But the bigger mistakes about network news belong to the conservatives, to the Republicans, and also to the network baiters, especially those sympathetic to Jesse Helms and his war against CBS. There is virtually no ideological bias on evening news. There is no partisan bias on evening news. There is bias against incumbents and frontrunners. But that is journalism, not partisanship.

And as for the conservative fear that news spin determines public opinion, or that news agenda determines public concern, that is almost as far from the truth as Helms' indictment of Dan Rather. Unless they bug the opposition party headquarters, leaders set policy agendas, not the press. In 1984, the only time spin really seemed to matter was when the networks decided to spin more critically against Gary Hart, the media phenomenon of the year. And that critical spin was, at the time, critical to Hart. But why should conservatives complain about that? Come to think of it, the Republicans have carried 93 states out of the last 100 in the Electoral College vote—more than 80 percent of the states since 1972. What's the beef?

We found the networks add a line or two of bad press to a day's campaign piece. And they will work double over-time to find evidence that tars the front-runner or incumbent with things as petty as obscene language or as potentially damaging as Watergate. But that's about all they do.

The 1980 election was a great election for those of us who believe liberal bias in the media is a near-myth. The networks covered left-leaning Kennedy more negatively than center-seeking Jimmy Carter. They covered Carter, the moderate, more negatively than right-of-center Reagan. And 1984 is a great election too, for those of us who believe that, in general elections especially, the network news programs and personnel are more a factor than a force: what they "do" is almost never enough to transform an election, unless "do" includes their coverage of facts, conditions, and real events.

Even for those who lost this election, there is some good news: In 1984, four reasonably responsible candidates spoke through three reasonably responsible networks to one reasonably responsible electorate. What need is there for conservatives to blame the networks, the Democrats to blame television, or the rest of us to blame the system? It was a pretty good show on network news in 1984, and it was even a little bit more than that.

☑

1 For a more complete discussion of these scores and their impact see Michael J. Robinson, "Where is the Beef? Media and Media Elites in '84," in Austin Ranney, *The American Elections of 1984*, American Enterprise Institute, Washington, D.C., forthcoming 1985.

2 Ibid. For Bush and for Ferraro, Caddell's measures are more or less biweekly.

3 On three public occasions since the election, Mondale has made reference to his free media performance, what that performance cost him personally, and what that performance portends for American democracy.

4 The ABC Viewpoint surveys, begun in 1981 and conducted with the express purpose of gauging public attitudes toward TV news, find that the overwhelming majority of the American people see no partisan bias on evening news. When asked if "television news reports tend to favor the Democratic party or Republican party," 67% said neither party, 17% the Democrats, and 11% the Republicans. On the other hand, 35% saw "television news reporters as pro-Communist in their views." See Viewpoint Poll, #8, June 15-19, 1984, ABC Survey #0121.

5 CBS, in fact, often turns up being the "conservative" network. See Michael J. Robinson, "Jesse Helms, Take Stock," *Washington Journalism Review*, April 1985.

6 The 826 stories were of the following types: presidential and vice-presidential campaign reports, 698 pieces; "lower level" campaign reports, 31 pieces; "official" reports about the president or vice-president (not linked to the campaign), 78 pieces; "other," 19 pieces.

7 William C. Adams, "The Media in Campaign '84: Convention Coverage," *Public Opinion*, December/January 1985.

8 ABC presented three pieces in a row on October 9, all dealing with the age issue.

9 William Greider, "Terms of Endearment: How the News Media Came to be All the President's Men," *Rolling Stone*, December 20, 1984.

10 Michael J. Robinson and Margaret A. Sheehan, *Over the Wire and on TV: CBS and UPI in Campaign '80*, Russell Sage, New York, 1983, passim.

11 Our surveys in April 1984 show that almost two thirds of the American public did not know why Ed Meese had been in the news at the time; half could not identify him. Michael J. Robinson and Maura Clancey, "Teflon Politics," *Public Opinion*, April/May 1984.

by Laurily Epstein and Gerald Strom

Survey Research and Election Night Projections

The passage of time has done nothing to abate criticisms of network projections of Ronald Reagan's victory before polls closed on the West Coast. The visceral reactions that immediately followed the election have been replaced by empirical studies, but the battle is no less intense. Evidence may have supplanted emotionalism, but the aim is the same: to demonstrate that would-be voters were, in fact, dissuaded from voting by the early evening projections.

No one has argued that the projections were incorrect or that they somehow "cheated" Jimmy Carter of a second term in the White House. Instead, the accusation is that early evening projections reduce turnout, and that, in turn, affects contests below the presidency.

The issue remains unresolved, despite a spate of studies going back to the 1964 election, which have found that early evening projections have no systematic effect on turnout.[1] Although the early studies used survey data, the sample sizes were so small that the results have been questioned on those grounds alone. The more recent studies have used aggregate data—and are challenged on those grounds—or have used survey data—but have suffered from trying to compare presidential and midterm electorates.

For example, a study we did, published in 1981, looked at turnout from 1960 to 1980 (a period characterized by alternating early evening and late night election projections) by using total votes cast as the numerator and the voting age population as the denominator.[2] It showed that early evening projections did not diminish turnout on the West Coast, at least when compared to turnout trends elsewhere in the country. This study has been criticized on the grounds that it is risky to speculate about individual behavior from aggregate data.

A recently published study also used aggregate data, but with California's registered voters as the denominator and ballots cast on election day (absentees were excluded) as the numerator, and showed that turnout on the West Coast *was* affected by the 1980 projections.[3] But California's registration procedures changed in the mid-1970s, and this may have led to an artificially inflated base of registered voters by 1980.

A study using survey data from the Census in 1972 and 1974 showed that, in 1972, turnout on the West Coast was affected by the early evening projection.[4] This study suffers from two problems. First, it compares presidential and midterm electorates. Second, it indulged in a little projection of its own—using data from the 1972 and 1974 elections to speculate about 1980.

Because voting decisions are made by individuals, there are those who insist that survey data are the only appropriate source of information about potential media effects on turnout. But until 1980, there were no reliable survey data available to address this issue.

In January of 1981, however, the Survey Research Center at the University of Michigan reinterviewed two of their national election samples, asking a series of questions designed to determine the effects of early projections (and Carter's early concession speech) on voting behavior. Both were stratified random samples of the adult population in some of the 48 mainland states. Of the original 2,579 respondents in the two samples, about 1,800 (69 percent) completed the January telephone interview. This drop in the number of respondents from an otherwise representative national sample is a serious problem with the data. The author of a series of papers based on the data acknowledges that the January 1981 sample is neither random nor representative.[5] These data are, however, the best currently available.

The questions asked of the respondents included: whether or not they had voted; the time of day they had voted (or decided not to vote); their reasons for not voting if they had abstained; and several questions about the time of day they had first heard reports or projections of election results. Because these respondents were a subset of the entire national sample, their responses could be matched with Michigan's vote validation project, which used official voting records to determine whether each respondent was registered to vote and whether the respondent actually voted. Vote validation was critical because voting rates determined by surveys are routinely higher than actual rates. We used only the validated vote in our analysis.

Jackson's Research

John Jackson, the principal investigator of the January 1981 survey, has presented at least three papers analyzing these same data.[6] Using some fairly sophisticated statistical modeling techniques, Jackson asserts that some combination of election night news broadcasts, the early evening projections, and Carter's concession speech lowered overall turnout by 6 to 12 percent. We believe that there are a number of very serious problems with Jackson's methodology and analysis.

First, he reports that there were 1,814 respondents in the survey, but we could find only 1,800 in the tapes furnished by the University of Michigan. Similarly, he excluded respondents for whom there was not complete data, but does not tell the reader what constitutes missing information. Thus, it is unclear how he arrived at the 1,123 respondents used in his analysis.

Second, there are problems with his recoding and collapsing of variables. For example, he assumes that all polls closed at 8:00 p.m. local time,[7] yet a majority did *not* in 1980. All or parts of twenty-two states closed their polls before 8:00 p.m., twenty-two states and the District of Columbia closed at 8:00 p.m., and all or parts of only five states closed after 8 p.m.

Jackson's findings of reduced turnout are based on model estimates that assess the likelihood of individuals voting before or after 6 p.m. local time (when he believes people nationwide could have heard election news). But since it was less likely for polls to close at 8:00 p.m., the probability Jackson assigns for voting after 6:00 p.m. is undoubtedly incorrect—network projections or no network projections.

Moreover, it appears that he used three time zones instead of four. Additionally, he asserts that the South and the East are on Eastern time, the Midwest is on Central time, and the West is on Pacific time.[8] (There is no reference to the Mountain region, so we are forced to infer that it falls into "the West.") Yet five of the eleven former Confederate states are wholly or partly in a time zone other than Eastern, and large areas of what are typically considered the Midwest are on Eastern, not Central, time. And, of course, Mountain states are on Mountain, not Pacific, time.

This lack of specificity regarding time zones and regions may help to account for the peculiar regional coefficients Jackson reports in his various studies.

Third, Jackson uses one model to estimate the likelihood of voting and then uses these results to project turnout. Thus, he compounds normal error in the measurement of variables with additional error in model estimation. Thus, it is very unclear what he is estimating or what the true values of the parameters really are.

A Different Methodology

We steered away from sophisticated statistical models, and looked instead at the actual data collected by Michigan. First, we excluded from their sample respondents who were not registered to vote (22 respondents). We allowed in our pool those who were registered and those for whom registration information was missing or incomplete. This increased the pool of eligible nonvoters —but not the pool of voters—and we may therefore be overstating the numbers who did not vote because of early forecasts. In the end, there were 1,778 respondents in the sample.

These respondents divided neatly into three groups: those who had voted (1,047); those who had not voted (574); and those for whom there was missing information on vote validation (157).

Having identified these three categories of respondents, we tried to establish who might have been affected by election night broadcast information. To do this we used the Michigan respondents' answers to the following questions: 1. When did you vote? 2. If you didn't vote, did you ever intend to vote? 3. If you didn't vote, when did you decide not to vote? 4. If you didn't vote, why not? 5. When did you first hear news reports about the election?

We selected the most liberal question about hearing reports of election results, to bend over backward to make the case *for* a media impact.

The Sample

Because we were looking for the impact of election night coverage on those who might have voted but did not, we excluded from our sample the 1,047 respondents who had voted. This left us with 574 nonvoters. Unfortunately, 175 of those claimed to have voted, when in fact they had not; therefore, they could not have been asked the series of questions about why they did not vote. Excluding these missing cases left us with 399 respondents who had been asked the nonvoting questions. Of these, 143 (or 36 percent) stated that they had never intended to vote. Those who stated that they had intended to vote were asked when they had decided not to vote. Of these respondents, 98 said they had decided not to vote before election day, and 103 gave no answer to this question.

That brought us down to 45 respondents who had decided on election day not to vote, and so may have been affected by election night news. When asked for their reasons for abstaining, 41 of these 45 gave reasons other than election night news (e.g. illness, the weather). The remaining four respondents, however, stated they did not vote because they had heard that Carter had lost or was losing. Looked at in this way, election night news may have discouraged 1 percent (4/399) of registered nonvoters from voting. If these four voters had voted, the number of voters in the sample would have gone from 1,047 to 1,051 and the number of nonvoters would have declined from 574 to 570. This implies that actual turnout may have been decreased by 0.2 percent—in other words, if the four had voted, turnout would have been 0.2 percent higher than it was.

The Flaws

Although survey research is a well-accepted and popular tool, there are problems associated with analyzing its results. One is the inherent messiness of asking people to recall behavior which occurred several months (and in some cases, years) before the survey is conducted. This is true for all surveys that ask recall questions, including Jackson's.

Among the errors we found in Jackson's data are the following, determined by comparing responses from the January 1981 survey with the earlier Vote Validation Survey:

• Eight self-reported nonvoters from the post-election survey reported in January that they had voted, and even gave a time at which they had putatively voted.

• Three self-reported voters from the post-election survey reported in January that they had not voted.

• Seventy-four individuals reported in the January survey that they had not voted because they had not registered when, in fact, they had.

Thus, at least 5 percent of the sample is known to have given the wrong information about their registration or voting behavior. (This 5 percent overlaps, but not entirely, with the 175 January respondents—10 percent of the sample—who reported that they had voted when, in fact, they had not.) While such a modest misreporting has no particular effect on the entire survey analysis, it can have a devastating effect on the analysis of any given individual's behavior.

Jackson himself admits that there are two problems with his data set. First, he noted that the sample, while drawn from what was originally a set of random samples, is not random and, therefore, not representative of the original sample or of the adult population. Second, he noted that there was error in recall of both time of vote and time of hearing the news.

Our analysis of Jackson's data confirms that the sample was not random. It was skewed toward more upscale respondents. Since such people pay more attention to the media than the less affluent and less educated do, potential media effects are exaggerated by their over-inclusion. Indeed, this may explain why Jackson found that Republicans, not Democrats, were dissuaded from voting because of the coverage.

Our analysis of the data also substantiated Jackson's statement that there was a fair amount of misreporting of when news was heard; many people said they heard the news well before they could have. While we have no way to validate the time of vote, we assume that this, too, was subject to inaccuracy.

Conclusion

Our purpose here is not to challenge the integrity of survey research or to criticize the methodology employed by scholars at the University of Michigan. Instead, we wish to note that not all questions can be addressed adequately by survey methodology. The *magni-tude* of media effects on would-be voters is one of those questions. Using the same data—but with strikingly different methods—John Jackson found turnout reduced in 1980 by 6 to 12 percent because of election night coverage. We found four nonvoters, or 0.2 percent of all eligible respondents, who reported that they did not vote because of election night coverage. This discrepancy between Jackson's findings and our own illustrates the difficulties of trying to use survey data to measure the *magnitude* of media effects.

For those who believe that the difference between 0.2 percent and 6 to 12 percent is insignificant—merely the result of social scientists quibbling over arcane methodological niceties—it should be noted that a large number of people, including some legislators, believe that the networks should cease reporting election news until all polls are closed. Their argument is predicated on the assumption—backed up by data such as Jackson's—that election night projections reduce turnout and thereby interfere with the democratic process. Many people not only believe this—they feel legislation is needed to prohibit network projections.

The state of Washington, for example, recently passed a law banning any exit polling activity less than 300 feet from the polling place. While the law does not explicitly prohibit the practice, it makes it—and any predictions based on exit polls—almost impossible.

We do not believe that there is any evidence that election night news coverage has had a significant effect on turnout. Leaving aside any consideration of the First Amendment and concentrating instead on what are purported to be the facts involved, we see no reason for the networks to discontinue their policy of projecting winners when whatever data the news organizations have amassed allow them to do so. ☑

[1] K. Lang and G. Lang, "Ballots and Broadcasts: The Impact of Expectations and Election Day Perceptions of Voting Behavior," paper presented at the Annual Conference of the American Association for Public Opinion Research, 1965; D. A. Fuchs, "Election-Day Radio-Television and Western Voting," *Public Opinion Quarterly*, 30 (Summer 1966), 226-237; H. Mendelsohn, "Election-Day Broadcasts and Terminal Voting Decisions," *Public Opinion Quarterly*, 30 (Summer 1966), 212-225; W. Miller, "Analysis of the Effects of Election Night Predictions on Voting Behavior," Hearings of the Subcommittee on Communications, Committee on Commerce, U.S. Senate, 90th Congress (July 1967), 211-219.

[2] Laurily K. Epstein and Gerald S. Strom, "Election Night Projections and West Coast Turnout," *American Politics Quarterly*, 9 (October 1981), 479-491.

[3] Philip L. Dubois, "Election Night Projections and Voter Turnout in the West: A Note on the Hazards of Aggregate Data Analysis," *American Politics Quarterly*, 11 (July 1983), 349-364.

[4] R. Wolfinger and P. Linquiti, "Network Election Day Predictions and Western Voters," *Public Opinion* (February/March 1981), 56-60.

[5] John Jackson and William McGee, "Election Reporting and Voter Turnout," Report of the Center for Political Studies, The University of Michigan, Ann Arbor, 1981; John Jackson, "Election Reporting and Voter Turnout," Center for Political Studies, Institute for Social Research, The University of Michigan, Ann Arbor, 1982; John Jackson, "Election Night Reporting and Voter Turnout," *American Journal of Political Science*, 27 (November 1983), 615-635.

[6] Ibid.

[7] According to Jackson (1982), "We use poll closings of 8 PM local time for each region, assuming that the east and south are on Eastern time, the midwest on Central time and the west on Pacific time."

[8] Ibid.

Laurily Epstein is a polling consultant to NBC News. Gerald Strom is an associate professor of political science at the University of Illinois at Chicago.

by Nick Thimmesch

The Editorial Endorsement Game

Since 1932, *Editor & Publisher*, the newspaper industry's weekly journal, has polled the nation's dailies about their editorial support, or endorsements, for presidential nominees. Only once in all those elections did a majority favor the Democratic candidate—Lyndon B. Johnson when he ran against Senator Barry Goldwater in 1964. In that year, even the solidly Republican *New York Herald-Tribune* broke precedent and backed the Democrat.

In 1984, this longstanding pattern of newspaper endorsements of the GOP candidate again ran true to form. Of 714 papers responding to *E & P*'s survey, 394 were for Reagan, 76 backed Mondale, and 244 reported being "uncommitted" or "no endorsement." Of the papers polled, Reagan got 51.3 percent of the circulation, Mondale 22.2, and 27 percent were neutral. The *E & P* survey was the fourteenth it had conducted since 1932.

The *E & P*'s polling shows that in thirteen of those fourteen elections, the overwhelming majority of dailies supported the Republican candidate, though the Democrat won eight times. This record leads many political observers to shrug off newspaper endorsements as irrelevant. Is it fair to conclude that the *E & P* results show only that the majority of newspaper publishers are conservative businessmen who impose their presidential preferences on their editorial page editors or editorial boards?

The quick answer is yes, but there are notable exceptions and some fascinating aspects to the endorsement business. In this year's election, the *Miami Herald* endorsed President Reagan "with reservations," declaring his ticket superior to the Mondale-Ferraro team. But the *Herald* also published a column by editor Jim Hampton, who said most editorial board members wanted to recommend Mondale, and that the Reagan endorsement "represents Publisher Dick Capen's exercising of his authority to override the board's collegial decisions."

In 1968, the late Captain Harry Guggenheim, then president of *Newsday*, had his paper endorse Richard M. Nixon. His publisher, Bill D. Moyers, a Democrat,

disagreed, so Guggenheim graciously allowed him to write an editorial endorsing Hubert H. Humphrey and ran it alongside the paper's official endorsement.

Nonalignment

If there is one trend in this game, it is for publishers and editors to split on the endorsement questions, either disagreeing on the candidates or on whether there should be an endorsement at all. The *Los Angeles Times* had an unbroken record of endorsing the G.O.P. candidate stretching from the nineteenth century to 1972. But since that election, the *Times* policy has been not to endorse, and it hasn't.

The *Baltimore Sun*, which had endorsed someone for every presidential race since 1936, decided not to endorse this year. Observed the *Sun*:

> We believe that in presidential elections, as in no others, there is an avalanche of information and commentary, of debate and analysis, that should satisfy the public's right to know. The voter has no need for the newspaper guidance that might be helpful in races for state and local office, for Congress, and in deciding ballot and judgeship questions.

The *Sun*'s decision grouped it with *E & P*'s fastest growing category, those papers expressing themselves as "uncommitted or undecided."

In 1932, *E & P* listed 511 dailies for the Democratic candidate, Franklin Delano Roosevelt, 656 for Republican Herbert Hoover, and 94 (8 percent) neutral. By 1940, with about the same number of dailies operating, 171 (13.5 percent) declared themselves uncommitted in the presidential race. By 1952, even with the popular "Ike" running, 18 percent of the dailies were neutral. Between 1952 and 1976, about one-fourth of the dailies designated themselves as neutral.

In 1980, with a third major candidate (John Anderson) in the race, a whopping 42 percent of the papers opted for the neutral stance, about as many as supported Ronald Reagan. But Reagan's 443 papers represented 48 percent of the circulation of those papers responding, and the 439 papers indicating "uncommitted" or "do not endorse," accounted for only 26 percent of the circulation.

Without checking the charts, some Republican partisans claim that while the majority of dailies have endorsed the Republicans over the years, the influential papers with big circulations have more often endorsed Democrats. The aggregate circulations of the smaller papers endorsing the G.O.P. candidates, they say, hardly matches that of the big papers.

The facts don't bear out such conjecture. In every election except 1964, the aggregate circulation of the dailies endorsing the Republican far exceeded that of the Democratic or third party candidate.

Editor & Publisher's findings for the 1932 and 1936 elections, which Roosevelt won by landslides, show that the majority of the dailies' aggregate circulation went for the Republican candidate.

In 1940, Willkie had 59 percent of the circulation endorsing him, compared with Roosevelt's 19 percent. In 1944, Dewey had 64 percent of the circulation, and FDR only 14 percent (22 percent were unannounced). In 1948, Dewey got 79 percent, compared to Harry S Truman's meager 10 percent.

Eisenhower swamped Adlai Stevenson by an 80-11 percent score on circulation in 1952, and 73-13 in 1956. Richard M. Nixon, no darling of editorial writers (but approved by many publishers), won endorsements from papers having 71 percent of the circulation in 1960, 70 percent in 1968, and 77 percent in 1972.

President Gerald R. Ford received 62 percent of the circulation in 1976, almost three times Carter's number. In 1980, Ronald Reagan's 48 percent represented a big drop for a Republican, but Jimmy Carter received only 22 percent. John Anderson had to scrape along on only 4 percent of the circulation.

Of the two papers regarded as the most influential, the *Washington Post* most often declared itself neutral. While favoring Republicans four times since 1932, the *Post* was neutral seven times, and backed Democrats three times—Lyndon Johnson (1964), Jimmy Carter (1980), and Walter Mondale (1984). As for the *New York Times*, the other big endorsement politicos yearn for, its support of Walter Mondale in 1984 marked the ninth time since 1932 that it had blessed a Democrat. Its Republican endorsements were for Wendell Willkie in 1940, Thomas E. Dewey in 1948, and Dwight Eisenhower in 1952 and 1956. The *Times* was neutral in 1944, when FDR made his bid for a fourth term.

Republican Media Elite?

Rare indeed is the politician who doesn't welcome and express gratitude for a newspaper endorsement. "When you get an endorsement for Mondale from prestigious papers like the *New York Times*, the *Philadelphia Inquirer*, the *Louisville Courier*, and the *St. Petersburg Times*, that carries weight," says Scott Widmeyer, deputy press secretary in the Mondale-Ferraro campaign.

But Widmeyer adds that "endorsements don't deliver votes." He is quite right. Consider the eight winning Democratic presidential candidates since 1932, and the weight of the editorial support for their opponents.

Franklin D. Roosevelt won large victories each time he ran—from the depth of the Great Depression through the worst of World War II—and each time his Republican opponent won a comfortable majority of those newspapers making endorsements or statements of support.

Harry S Truman was literally swamped in the endorsement game. Truman won approval from only 15 percent of the papers *E & P* polled, while Dewey won 65 percent. The largest, most powerful, and influential papers were for Dewey: the *New York Times*, the *New York Daily News*, the *Chicago Tribune*, every paper in Philadelphia, Cleveland, Detroit, and San Francisco. The list went on. The *Chicago Sun Times* backed Truman, but both St. Louis papers, including the Democratic-tilted *St. Louis Post-Dispatch*, favored Dewey.

John F. Kennedy had nearly as rough a time as Truman. Kennedy gleaned endorsements from only 16 percent of the circulation, whereas Nixon's endorsements came from 58 percent of the papers representing 71 percent of the circulation. Jimmy Carter was no favorite of publishers, either. His endorsements came from 12 percent of the papers with 23 percent of the circulation. In fact, in Carter's home state, Georgia, Ford won twelve daily newspaper endorsements, compared to Carter's eight. But in Michigan, Ford won 14 endorsements, and Carter got one—the *Detroit Free Press*.

The sole Democrat to win a majority of editorial endorsements was Lyndon B. Johnson. His contest with Goldwater moved a total of 445 dailies to endorse him, while his opponent, the New Apostle of Conservatism, got 368. It was apparently so difficult for publishers to endorse a Democrat that 238 marked themselves as Independent in 1964, and 639 indicated no choice in that lopsided election. Interestingly enough, many traditional Republican papers—the *New York Herald Tribune* and the *Washington Star* being prime examples—endorsed the 1964 Democratic nominee to protest the Goldwater candidacy. At that, Johnson got 62 percent of the circulation; Goldwater, 21; and 17 percent were uncommitted.

Democrats shouldn't be optimistic about acquiring presidential endorsements from the nation's dailies. But Republicans shouldn't expect to get their customary lopsided margins of support, either. With the present strong trend for papers to be neutral on presidential endorsements, it is unlikely in the near future that G.O.P. candidates will enjoy the 80 percent of the circulation support that Eisenhower did in 1952 (933 papers), or the 77 percent that Nixon did in 1972.

The Kings and the Power

Newspapers have simply become less partisan and predictable. A look at *E & P*'s compilations shows that a large majority of dailies in the South consistently backed Roosevelt and then Truman, when he ran in 1948. Even publishers in the Old Confederacy harbored misgivings about Yankee Republicans until Eisenhower and Nixon came along.

In recent elections, the majority of Southern papers have endorsed the Republicans. The *Atlanta Constitution*, unequaled as a major voice in that region, is a notable exception. It has endorsed the Democratic nominee in twelve of the fourteen presidential elections since 1932. This year, it was right in form, and endorsed Mondale.

There was a time when a "chain" or "group" of newspapers followed the divinely issued order from its president or president/tycoon on whom to endorse. Thus, the Hearst newspapers, on orders from William Randolph Hearst, enthusiastically backed FDR in 1932. But by 1936, Bill Hearst was disillusioned with his hero. The word went out to endorse Landon, and the obedient Hearstling editors did.

As long as Colonel Robert R. McCormick was publisher of the *Chicago Tribune*, there was no need to look at the editorial page for the presidential endorsement. It was automatically Republican. Nowadays, the *Tribune* endorses many Democrats for state and local offices, and its endorsements of Republican presidential aspirants are often tentative.

In endorsing Reagan in 1984, the *Tribune* criticized his "refusal to accept a linkage between the federal deficit and economic instability as threatening to bankrupt America and severely damage the free world economy." The *Tribune* also said Reagan's "ignorance" about the Soviet Union and his "air-headed" rhetoric on foreign policy issues was an "embarrassment" to the U.S. and "a danger to world peace." Some endorsement. The *Tribune* explained that it favored Reagan only because his philosophy of government results in less government growth, hence, less government intrusion than would Walter Mondale's.

The Chicago Tribune Co. owns several other papers, therefore it is a group. But there is no telling whom these other papers would endorse, because each has editorial autonomy. The same holds true for even larger collections of dailies owned by Gannett, Newhouse, Knight-Ridder, Times-Mirror, and Scripps-Howard. Once, Gannett's papers seemed to endorse the Republican presidential candidate uniformly, but no more.

The McClatchey newspaper group, particularly its "Bee" papers in California, have steadfastly endorsed the Democratic nominee. Thus, they are an anomaly.

Plenty of Nothing

One wonders why newspapers endorse at all? After all, there must be some discomfiture when the newspaper is out of tune with the electorate, and that is the case more often than not. The *New York Times* has ridden with seven winners and the same number of losers since 1932, but right or wrong, it is the *New York Times* speaking.

The reason newspapers continue the practice probably lies in the deep-rooted notion that an industry protected by the First Amendment should express its opinion on public interest matters, including the selection of the president.

"Newspapers endorse as part of their watchdog role," says John Consoli, who monitors endorsements as *E & P*'s news editor. "They feel they watch candidates and campaigns closer than the public does, and therefore have more insight into the election. They feel they are a mediator between the voters and the candidates, and should express their opinion.

"We compile their endorsements as a service to the industry. Publishers are a lot like little kids on this—they want to see what other papers do, and they have a keen interest in our compilation. This year, for instance, there was a rumor going around publishers that the *New York Daily News* might endorse Mondale because its new publisher, James Hoge, leans that way. But the *News* endorsed Reagan."

Still, Consoli acknowledges that "newspaper endorsements don't carry that much weight. People are unlikely in this day and age to turn to the editorial to read the endorsement, and then vote that way. They did more of this years ago before television. Television forms their impressions of a candidate far more than any newspaper endorsement."

John Buckley, assistant press secretary of the Reagan-Bush campaign, agrees. "Few endorsements influence very many people," he says. "But a few endorsements can make a difference. I'm thinking of the *New York Daily News* because of its concentrated New York readership, and the *New York Times* because of its leadership among papers."

Scott Widmeyer, his counterpart at Mondale-Ferraro headquarters, says newspaper endorsements have been downgraded in impact just as all endorsements have, whether they come from labor unions, organizations, or prominent persons. "People are just more independent these days," he explains.

But hope always lurks in the hearts of even the most jaded politician, and an endorsement can light up that hope. Candidates' voices rise when they mention their endorsements, as if such publisher/editor support certifies and ordains them to the office they seek.

Then there is the claim by John P. Robinson, a University of Michigan journalism professor, that the overwhelming support Nixon received in 1968 by newspaper coverage and endorsements might well have elected him.

"The largely pro-Nixon coverage carried by the newspapers in 1968 was associated with some differential in the vote to the advantage of the Republican candidate."

Robinson's computations, based on a national probability sample of 1,346 Americans 21 years of age and older, showed that voters exposed to pro-Nixon newspapers were six percent less likely to vote for Humphrey, when several other determinants of the vote were held statistically constant.

While conceding that the public ranked television as its most important campaign news source, Robinson noted "far more report having voted for the candidate espoused by the newspaper than by the other media." Robinson concluded that newspapers had their greatest effect on the less committed. In the close election of 1968, the uncommitted vote was crucial.

When Nixon made his well-received speech to the American Society of Newspaper Editors last spring, he cracked that he had never had the media with him in a single election campaign. E & P immediately took issue, and cited the lopsided percentages of editorial support he had enjoyed in his three presidential campaigns. Nixon then clarified his observation (he didn't want to end this new honeymoon too quickly) by writing E & P that he was referring "primarily to television reporters and a number of newspaper reporters as well who took a different position from their publishers."

Ah, there's the rub, and perhaps Michigan's Professor Robinson should have made a clear distinction between endorsements and/or support, and day-to-day news coverage and editorial page treatment.

"We don't slant our news," the Washington Post's executive editor Ben Bradlee once said. "We just decide what to cover."

Indeed, a newspaper can focus on one or two dimensions of a candidate and his or her program, and thus provide coverage that the candidate will condemn as biased. The same newspaper's editorial page might also be hammering away at the candidate's views. But on the eve of the election, the publisher or even a majority of the editorial board members might reluctantly endorse that very same candidate.

Beyond Endorsements

Publishers are stellar members of the power establishment. They rub elbows with the top people in business and industry, as well as with educators, labor leaders, and even some social activists. But their exposure is nearly always with establishment people. Publishers also worry about the bottom line, and therefore view with considerable skepticism Democratic proposals claiming to rectify economic wrongs. Small wonder, then, that a majority of publishers consistently go for the Republican candidate.

Some go even beyond that. A small ruckus developed in the newspaper industry this fall over an organization of publishers, calling itself "Newspaper Friends of Reagan-Bush," which disseminated "informational materials" on the G.O.P. ticket to small dailies and weeklies.

"Newspaper Friends" was comprised of about 50 publishers of small community newspapers. It was headed by George Measer, head of Bee Publications and publisher of eight weeklies with a combined paid and free circulation of 35,000 in suburban Buffalo.

"I believe that people should be involved in the political process," said Measer, "and I've heard so many publishers complain about the political process, saying they're afraid of what might happen if Reagan didn't get it for another four years."

Well, before the uproar subsided, there were righteous warnings that the very freedom of the press was being jeopardized by these small-town publisher believers in Reagan-Bush; cherished editorial integrity was at stake. The best argument was that it is one thing for a publisher to endorse, and quite another to distribute campaign propaganda (informational materials) to a network of newspapers, however modest their circulations.

In any case, it is doubtful that "Newspaper Friends" swung the election—regardless of their endorsements and campaign materials.

Given the itch to express opinion that exists in the newspaper industry, the sense of power most publishers feel, and the horserace (tout sheet) aspect of American presidential elections, it is very likely that newspaper endorsements of presidential candidates will continue for a long time, even if their influence is negligible. ☑

PART THREE

Paid Advertisements in the General Election

by Edwin Diamond and Stephen Bates

The Media in Campaign '84

The Ads

The history of the 1984 presidential campaign advertising has already been written. It holds that Ronald Reagan was the beneficiary of a shrewd, slick marketing effort by his vaunted Tuesday Team of Madison Avenue all-stars, while Walter Mondale suffered from stumbling, fumbling media managers and his own discomfort on television ("I never warmed to TV, and it never warmed to me," Mondale said in a post-mortem).

In truth, almost as much creativity went into spinning this legend as went into the media campaign itself. The most important facts about advertising in the 1984 campaign are:

1. Some 70 political ads were aired, 50 by Reagan and 20 by Mondale. Another 60 were worked on but never shown.

2. Each candidate spent between $23 and $27 million in the general election campaign to make and air these ads.

3. Pervasive and stylish as these campaign images were, they actually did very little to alter the political realities of 1984. That is, Ronald Reagan began the year with a substantial lead over Walter Mondale in the presidential preference polls, and the needle stuck there for most of the rest of the year. None of the images put

forward by either campaign did much to change the numbers.

Mondale's Effort

Douglas Watts, the media director of the Reagan campaign, told us that Mondale's advertising was "confused, uneven, and poorly planned." From a technical standpoint, this is not so. Time-buying is one of the technologies of the campaign, and the Mondale people obviously mastered it well enough. In fact, the A. C. Nielsen Co. measurements—the Holy Ratings that Madison Avenue worships—clearly show that Mondale had the superior time-buying operation. Clever placement of his five-minute spots meant Mondale enjoyed more viewers per dollar than Reagan. A Mondale spot on CBS on October 4, for example, drew a 19.0 rating—the best political rating of the month—while a Reagan spot rated an 8.8—the worst of the month—on NBC the following night. The Mondale problem was not advertising technique but political judgment.

Another of the conventional criticisms of the Mondale media campaign holds that it was "themeless and visionless," to use the phrase of Phil Dusenberry, a

Tuesday Team all-star and creative director at Batten, Barton, Durstine & Osborn, Inc. (BBD&O) in New York. (Dusenberry did the Michael Jackson campaign for Pepsi and Reagan's 18-minute waving-fields-of-flags docu-spot at the Republican convention last August.) Again, the reality is that the Mondale campaign did have a theme and a vision; as it happened, they were the wrong ones.

Mondale's senior media adviser was Richard Leone, who has a background in New Jersey politics. The Mondale spot maker was Roy Spence, a youthful advertising man from Austin, Texas. The media people reported in turn to "the Norwegians"—the somewhat invidious term for the small band of Minnesota loyalists around Mondale. Quite early in the race, internal campaign documents and memos show, Mondale policy makers decided to make a major issue out of the national debt and the Reagan administration's presumed inability to deal with it. A Democratic strategist remembers hearing a top Mondale media man declare: "We're going to make Reagan eat the deficit."

Economic issues and the need for a tax increase were the Mondale themes—recall the candidate brandishing all those tax bracket flip charts. But, as George Will suggested, not even Sir Laurence Olivier at his most mellifluous could have sold a tax hike to the voters of 1984. Still, the deficit spots weren't bad. One ad cited $1,800 as your "share of Mr. Reagan's deficit," and ended with the line, "Let's stop mortgaging America." Another ad showed legions of blue-suited men walking out of the Treasury building and into waiting limos. The voice-over identified them as "profitable corporations that pay no taxes, defense contractors on bloated budgets, foreign interests who make money on our debt." Another Mondale economic ad showed elderly women. Asked about further food stamp cuts, one of them shakes her head and says, almost in a whisper, "No way. No way." Another woman says, "I just want enough to get along. That's all I ask." While some of Reagan's media men judged that Mondale's best ad, its theme (Reagan's unfairness) never took off.

The Mondale media effort, then, was not short of technical talent. David Sawyer and Scott Miller, who did John Glenn's polished, state-of-the-art ads during the early primaries—those ads equating Glenn with the values of the heartland and the possibilities of tomorrow—also created more than a dozen spots for Mondale. Most of those were what the trade calls "intense reality" spots on such topics as toxic waste and nuclear war. Only one, featuring a roller coaster, was aired. "Nineteen eighty-two," the voice-over begins, as the roller coaster plunges down a steep slope, "Reaganomics sinks our country into the deepest recession and unemployment in fifty years." The ad closes with the roller coaster plunging again, and the message: "If you're thinking of voting for Ronald Reagan in 1984, think of what will happen in 1985."

Sawyer and Miller and their firm, D.H. Sawyer

Associates, came to work for Mondale well after the basic economic themes had been laid down by "the Norwegians." David Garth, the New York media man, had been invited to join up in the interval between the thematic formulation and the arrival of Sawyer, et al. But Garth had insisted upon full control of the media campaign, a prerogative Mondale's inner circle would not yield. After this well-publicized episode, Garth sat out the fall presidential race. It wasn't so much that the Mondale media effort was disorganized, as the popular accounts had it; the effort was organized, but in non-media hands.

The Reagan Approach

Similarly, reality looks quite different when the Reagan campaign is stripped of its legends. The Tuesday Team's higher-priced spread of advertising talents, outwardly so smooth and competent, just barely managed to conceal its true *lumpen* nature.

As the GOP campaign began, Nancy Reagan and Michael Deaver engineered the ousting of Peter Dailey, the *Los Angeles Times* adman who had done Reagan's 1980 ads. The main objection was that Dailey's work had looked amateurish. The White House then bypassed traditional Republican political media firms—Robert Goodman in Baltimore, Douglas Bailey and John Deardourff in Washington—and decided to create its own ad agency, the Tuesday Team. Doug Watts, a political consultant from Sacramento, was brought in as media director to manage the team and work as liaison between the campaign and the White House. Jim Travis of Della Femina, Travisano and Partners, New York, became Tuesday Team head, presiding over what he called "the greatest collection of all-star creative people ever assembled." Team members included—besides Phil Dusenberry—Hal Riney, the writer and the voice behind Gallo wine ads, and Ron Travisano, creator of the Meow Mix singing cat.

The Tuesday Team's debut came in late May. The first flight of ads featured what would become trademarks of the Reagan TV campaign: bubbly optimism and patriotism ("It's morning again in America"); technically lush photography and editing; low-key music and voice-overs; and, in many of the spots, only a momentary glance of the candidate (Reagan appeared only in the closing graphic in the early ads, in a still photo alongside a flag). The press's knee-jerk reaction: the spots were too slick. But, as Watts told us, "The slickness was a very conscious decision. We wanted high production values. Number one, Nancy Reagan demanded them, and we wanted to serve her demands. Number two, the Tuesday Team people would never do it any other way. And number three, that's always been my political advertising strategy. People don't want to watch any commercial, especially not a political one. You have to fit your message into the context of the medium."

As to the decision to keep Ronald Reagan out of

the early ads, Watts says it was part of the early counter-programming. "The Democrats were running around screaming at each other," he told us. "We wanted to remain above the fray, and the best way to do that was in third person. There were times when the Great Communicator was the best tool and times when he wasn't." Watts also says that Reagan, "a very humble man," refused to appear in any spot that praised him too lavishly.

The costs of making the "Morning Again" spots were high, partly because of the lavish production and partly because of Reagan's union past. Most political campaigns get signed release forms from people who appear in their ads, in exchange for a one-time fee. The Reagan campaign felt that that wouldn't do, because Reagan had served six terms as the president of the Screen Actors Guild. Instead, the campaign paid some $450,000 in residuals to the people in its spots—a specified fee each time the spot was aired.

Grizzly Details

After the May flight, the Tuesday Team went off the air, with the exception of Dusenberry's 18-minute convention piece. Stuart Spencer, the California political strategist working with Reagan, suggested some attack ads to highlight the divisive Democratic primaries, to be aired around the time of the Democratic convention. One set of ads was produced from primary footage, showing Gary Hart, Jesse Jackson, John Glenn, and Reubin Askew criticizing Mondale. But, with polls showing Reagan so far in front, the idea was believed to be too heavy-handed and was scrapped. In the end, most of the material never left the can.

Despite Reagan's steady lead in the polls, the campaign did end up airing a few negative ads. "I've never been in a campaign where you didn't have to take a few swift kicks at your opponent," says Watts. Perhaps the Tuesday Team's best negative spot was called "Tax Vignettes." It showed a hard-hat laborer, a housewife in a kitchen (trying to stretch the last of the mayonnaise to cover three sandwiches, while children yell and squabble all around), and a farmer working in the field. The announcer said that Mondale expects people to work more overtime, to stretch the family budget further, and to toil a few more hours each night on the farm —in order to pay higher taxes. The spot aired heavily for about two weeks, beginning a few days before the first debate.

For all the praise (and self-congratulation) of the Tuesday Team, it proved to be a Big Spender of the kind conservatives are supposed to disdain. On two different occasions, according to two campaign officials, the Madison Avenue boys "threw away" upwards of $100,000 on sappy spots—mercifully never aired after the White House and Watts saw them. The Tuesday Team ultimately produced forty-nine spots and a half-hour film, at a total cost of $27 million. Another thirty or so commercials were produced but not aired, and nearly 100

more spots were written but never produced.

For that matter, the most important Reagan spots were not the acclaimed good-feelings and waving-flags life style productions, but the straight stuff used right after the debate. The idea was simple: Let Reagan be Reagan. As one Republican campaign insider, admittedly no admirer of the Tuesday Team, said: "Following the first debate, we had to show that Reagan was upright, in charge, with all his abilities intact. Reagan on camera for as many appearances as possible was the ticket."

That postdebate period was one of the times when Reagan might have been vulnerable to opportunistic, aggressive Mondale media pressure. And indeed, confidential memos we've seen show that some strategists in the Mondale campaign foresaw the possibility of a strong Mondale showing in the first debate. Sawyer and Miller, for example, wanted to have a series of "citizen-reaction" interviews ready to go the morning after. These quick-strike spots would look very much like the networks' own postdebate reports. The Mondale media decision makers rejected the idea.

And then came the Tuesday Team's bear.

(Camera up on a grizzly, lumbering across a hilltop, crossing a stream, forging through underbrush. A drum plays incessantly, like a heartbeat, over ominous chords.)

Announcer (Hal Riney): There's a bear in the woods. For some people, the bear is easy to see. Others don't see it at all. Some people say the bear is tame. Others say it is vicious and dangerous. Since no one can really be sure who's right, isn't it smart to be as strong as the bear?

(The bear walks slowly along a ridge, silhouetted against the sky; it looks up, stops suddenly and takes a step backward. The camera pulls back to show a man standing a few yards away, facing the bear. A gun is slung over his shoulder. He too is silhouetted.)

Announcer: If there is a bear.

Closing graphic: "President Reagan: Prepared for Peace."

The idea was Riney's. He drew up a story board, using cutouts from magazines, and offered it for the first White House presentation. It was filmed in Oregon in May, with Riney directing by telephone; he was in Ireland at the time. The production cost (including the trained bear, which was taught to stop, look up, and step backward when it walked into a hidden wire) was about $80,000.

In high-tech campaigns like 1984's, extensive testing of spots is routine. After production, the bear ad was shown to no fewer than 100 focus groups. The campaign also aired the spot in a few markets and then telephoned viewers to see if they remembered it. Interviewers got a 75 percent recall; 50 percent recall is considered high. In all, the bear was probably the most heavily tested political spot in American history.

In our own work analyzing political advertising, published earlier this year (*The Spot: The Rise of Political Advertising on Television*, MIT Press), we discovered that the modern TV-ad campaign follows distinct stages, as predictable as kabuki theater. The stages usually conform to a campaign's chronology, and 1984 pretty much fit our general classification scheme. Phase one "identification" spots are designed to give the voter a sense of the candidate. They are followed by the "arguments" spots, which provide a view of what the candidate stands for. The ads in this stage of the campaign are not too specific (old ones had John Wayne endorsing Republican candidates and Henry Fonda supporting his son-in-law, Tom Hayden), and they are often designed for emotional appeal. Carroll O'Connor, for example, in his 1980 ads for Ted Kennedy, managed to convey working-class solidarity with the candidate. Argument spots, though, can also convey some of the candidate's major ideas or themes.

Phase three spots are "attack" spots, and they have had a genesis of their own. Contrary to popular belief, there is very little that is new about this kind of negative advertising. In 1952, Ike compared the Democrats to reckless drivers in an early negative ad. During the sixties and early seventies, the candidates themselves delivered the attacks, but by the late seventies, the attacks were usually delegated to the candidate's surrogates.

Phase four, what we call "I see an America . . .,"
usually concludes the campaign, though this year front-runner Reagan struck a positive attitude long before his challenger. For Mondale the phase four theme was still an attack—fear for the nation's fate—as Reagan continued with "feel good" and hope.

On the weekend before the election, the Mondale campaign heavily aired a five-minute spot, summoning images of nuclear war. The ad—placed in and around shows with high-Yuppie concentrations—employed the song "Teach Your Children" by Crosby, Stills, Nash, and Young, as the video cut back and forth from young children looking up in fear to missiles being launched. In the GOP's final spot, meanwhile, Reagan told voters: "With youth back in charge, we've turned the corner."

Hype, of course, is the price we pay in advertising and in politics. Not surprisingly, the ads we saw in 1984 weren't nearly as bad as critics claimed, nor were they as good as the media makers sometimes boasted. In all, we found, presidential campaign advertising was a sideshow to the election and not the main event. Real-world factors—incumbency, a voting class that saw itself at peace and prosperous, candidate debates that first stirred and then allayed apprehensions—were much more important in shaping the outcome. The voters loved Reagan in November as much as they had in January, and $50 million in TV advertising was just so much background music to the affair. ☞

U.S. Elections: Really a Bargain?

by Howard R. Penniman

A recent magazine article asserted that "other Western democracies conduct their elections at a much lower cost" than the United States. But the author provided no evidence except his estimate of the probable cost of a single senatorial election still six months away and a few words about the high price of American television network advertising. If examined reasonably, American elections are usually less expensive than those of other countries.

U.S. Elections

The Census Bureau reported that in November 1980, 164,381,000 residents in the United States were eighteen years of age or older. If we deduct from that the 6,343,000 residents who were not citizens, and another 460,000 who were in penal or mental institutions (though under state laws some confined persons are actually eligible to vote), there were 157,778,000 potential voters in the United States in 1980. They outnumbered the eligible electorate in Germany, Italy, or the United Kingdom by more than three and one-half to one, eligible Canadians by ten to one, Venezuelans by twenty to one, Israelis by more than seventy to one, and Irish by ninety to one. So, it would be strange indeed if the *total* cost of American election campaigns did not exceed the campaign costs in countries where voting populations are much smaller. If, however, we pro rate the election costs according to the number of potential voters, we can make reasonable comparisons.

According to Herbert E. Alexander, a leading American authority on campaign finance, in 1979-1980 it cost $239 million to elect the Congress and $275 million to elect the president. Both figures include the primary and general elections. The cost per eligible voter was $1.51 for the congressional campaign and $1.74 for the presidential campaign—a combined cost of $3.25 per eligible voter.

Congressional expense reports did not separate primary and general election costs, but the 1980 presidential primary and general election accounts showed the following: primaries and caucuses, $112.1 million; national conventions, $9.3 million; general elections, $142 million; and something called "miscellaneous and out-of-pocket expenses," $10.7 million. These figures included money raised and spent by people who were controlled by neither the candidates nor the parties.

Special Considerations

At least two institutional differences increase the cost of American electoral campaigns. The vast majority of radio and television stations in the United States are privately owned, for one thing, so American politicians and parties must buy time if they wish to send their message to the public by the most effective media. Doing so may account for as much as two-thirds of a party's national campaign expenditures. In all other Western democracies, the state owns all or most television and radio outlets. Parties have traditionally been granted free broadcast time for their electoral campaigns. Where there are privately owned stations, national rules usually require that political telecasts on government stations must be carried at the same time on the nongovernmental stations, at no cost to the political parties. More than three-fourths of the European democracies do not allow parties to purchase advertising time on state or private television or radio. The cost of the "free" time is, of course, ultimately paid by taxpayers.

The second institutional difference that affects election costs is the method used to select the head of state and the chief executive. In parliamentary democracies the head of state is either an hereditary monarch, a governor-general as in the Commonwealth countries, or a legislatively selected president. These heads of state have carefully defined

and limited powers. The chief executive is the prime minister, who is not elected by the voters but is generally chosen by the party or coalition that commands majority support in one or both houses of parliament. Only in France, Venezuela, and the United States has a president—who is both head of state and chief executive—been chosen by popular vote consistently over the last twenty-five years. Clearly, selection by popular vote entails enormously greater expenditures than selection by the majority in the national legislature.

France and Venezuela

French and American national elections are quite similar in many respects. Voters in both countries may participate twice in selecting the president and the legislators. In France, voters choose from among ten or a dozen contenders in the first round—much like an American primary. Unless one candidate receives an absolute majority in the first round, the two leading contenders face a runoff contest—the second round. The winner becomes the next president of France. A similar two-round process takes place when voters choose members of the chamber of deputies.

Unfortunately, while the French and American electoral processes are similar, French campaign financing data is virtually impossible to come by. A distinguished French political scientist gave up an opportunity to write a chapter on campaign financing in 1981 because, he said, "there is scant hope of ascertaining the truth [about campaign expenditures] . . . [I]t seems to me to be beyond the capacity of a single researcher."

In Venezuela, the situation is somewhat more promising. Venezuelans elect their president and their national and state legislators every five years in a manner that vaguely resembles the American system. The president and the legislators are voted on separately but, with the exceptions noted below, the party leaders rather than the rank and file choose the candidates. One of the major parties, the Acción Democratica (AD), twice conducted its own primary elections allowing all party members to participate in the selection of the party's presidential candidate. On both occasions, the intraparty battle for the nomination was so bitter that most analysts believe it was a factor in the party's defeat in the general election. In 1983, the AD held a limited primary in which only 17,315 party leaders participated. Other Venezuelan parties have never experimented with the primary system.

Reports of campaign expenditures are not required by Venezuelan law. It is possible, however, to secure reasonably accurate estimates of election costs from long-time students of Venezuelan elections who have also participated as campaign advisers. Reports by AEI authors state that in 1978 the AD alone spent $88 million, while expenditures of all parties may have reached $180 million. Preliminary estimates by some of the same experts placed the 1983 election costs at $200 million, which would mean an expenditure for each of the 7,589,000 eligible voters of approximately $26.35. The Venezuelan figures include the cost of advertisements on private television networks but not the free time on the public networks. If American political parties had spent at the same rate for each eligible voter, the total cost in 1980 would have exceeded $4 billion.

Reporting Requirements

Campaigns to elect members of national legislatures, whether congressmen or members of parliament, are sufficiently similar that their costs per eligible voter can be compared. Unfortunately, these must be limited to parliamentary elections for which there is either hard data or general agreement among country specialists on the cost of campaigns.

Khayyam Zev Paltiel suggests that the United States, unlike most democracies, "places heavy stress on the constraining value of publicity, [and] mandates some of the most elaborate reporting procedures at both the federal and state levels" to be found anywhere in the world. By contrast, some Scandinavian countries require no reports on campaign receipts and expenditures. The Norwegian and Swedish governments, according to Paltiel, believe that such reports "constitute a potential violation of the voters' right to privacy,

secrecy of the ballot, and the parties' right to internal autonomy and freedom from interference." The governments also believe that including a donor's name in a report can lead either to persecution or preferential treatment. The Netherlands, some of whose citizens compare themselves with their Scandinavian neighbors, likewise require no reporting on campaign financing.

The Australian parliament retreated from its previously very limited reporting in 1980 when a minor party leader, Don Chipp, threatened to challenge the election of anyone who failed to abide by campaign financing laws so unrealistic that politicians had largely ignored them since their adoption in 1927. The parliament answered the threat by simply repealing the law, leaving the country with no campaign financing regulation for the first time since 1902.

Less than adequate data are available on the real costs of campaigns in the United Kingdom and some Commonwealth countries. The difficulty arises in large measure because (a) the prime minister may call an election with as little as three weeks notice so the political parties must always be ready for a campaign; (b) the law strictly limits candidate expenditures at the constituency level during the brief campaign period; and (c) the national party, which is the center of modern British campaigns, is not required to report its expenditures. The "routine," but campaign-related, expenditures between elections are not included in reports on expenses submitted by the candidates or the parties. The total listed campaign costs of the four larger parties in 1983 amounted to just slightly more than $.50 per eligible voter. In addition to the absence of related precampaign data, that figure includes neither free broadcast time nor other subsidies-in-kind that the parties receive from the government or national party expenditures.

Ireland

The voters of Ireland select the members of the country's popularly elected branch, the Dail, by a proportional representation system known as the single transferable vote (STV). Three to five representatives are elected from each of more than forty districts. The electoral system often encourages competition not only between the parties but even between candidates within the same party. One result of this has been considerable spending at both the local

and the national levels.

In a generally typical election contest in 1981 the costs for the three largest parties at the national level were: Fianna Fail, £1,200,000; Fine Gael, £600,000; and Labour £93,000 of which £50,000 had been contributed by the Socialist Group in the Parliament of Europe.

Responses of the leaders of the major parties concerning local expenditures by their own party and the two opposition parties suggest that Fianna Fail and Fine Gael spent about the same at both the national and local levels. The leaders thought that Labour had spent only a third as much locally. Accepting those estimates, the constituency expenditures for the three parties would amount to £1,831,000. The total for both would be £3,724,000. In American dollars the amount would be $6,614,920. The cost for each of the 1,734,379 eligible voters would therefore have been $3.93. The cost of television is not included in the figures for Ireland.

Canada

After enduring years of widespread criticism of their freewheeling methods of raising and spending campaign funds, the Canadian parliament passed comprehensive regulations that came into effect in August 1974, just after the general elections. The new law recognized political parties as legal entities, required officers responsible for party activities to register, limited spending by both the central party and the candidate, and prohibited party advertising prior to the last four weeks of national political campaigns.

Parties and candidates meeting necessary legal requirements can now be reimbursed for a portion of their costs during the campaign. Private contributions to registered parties are encouraged by giving tax credits ranging from $75 (Canadian) for the first $100 contribution to a limit of $500 for a contribution of $1,150 and more. In 1980 American currency, these rebates would have ranged from $64.16 to $427.65.

The first elections conducted under the new rules took place in May 1979 and February 1980. The relative costs of the two campaigns were quite similar. In 1980, the total general election expenditure by the central parties and the candidates was $26,592,095 (Canadian)—$1.43 (American) for each of the 15,890,416 eligible voters. This amounted to $.08 per eligible voter less than was spent in the United States to cover the cost of primary and general elections for both houses of Congress. (Members of the Canadian senate are appointed, not elected.) The Canadian figures do not include the cost of the free time given on television and radio to registered parties, or precampaign expenditures for opinion surveys commissioned by the parties, or other expenditures made in anticipation of the official campaign.

The Federal Republic of Germany

The West German government heavily subsidizes the national political parties and the party-related foundations. Any party that won at least .5 percent of the total valid vote in the 1983 elections, for example, received 4.5 Deutsche Marks (DM) or approximately $1.85 (American) for each vote the party won. In 1983, the combined vote for the qualified parties was 38,303,805, which was worth about $71,658,230 in government subsidies. Longtime observers point out that private funding of the parties is encouraged with generous tax credits (one reason, they believe, that the total spending probably reaches about twice the government subsidy). Based on that estimate, the campaign cost for each of the 44,068,741 persons eligible to vote in the 1983 election would have been about $3.20—more than double the cost per eligible voter in the 1980 American congressional election. The German figures exclude free television and radio time, govern-

ment subsidies for foundations that provide research for the parties, and subsidies for parties at the state level.

The 1977 Israeli Elections

The 1977 Israeli elections were conducted under spending rules developed in 1973; with modest changes, these rules remained in effect through 1981. The rules called for more than the usual care in reporting, so post-1973 figures are generally more precise than earlier numbers. In 1977, according to Professor Leon Boim, all Israeli parties spent a total of IL97,092,381, at a time when the pound was worth $.10 American. The cost in American currency, then, was $9,709,238, or $4.34 for each of the 2,236,293 eligible voters in the country. This figure is nearly three times the per eligible voter cost for the 1980 congressional election in the United States; it also exceeds the combined costs of the congressional and presidential elections that year.

Conclusions

Calculating campaign costs on the basis of expenditures for eligible voters makes it possible to compare costs for units that are identical in all democracies. Comparing the absolute costs of campaigns in different countries only points up the obvious fact that it is more expensive to send messages to many people than to a few.

The cost per eligible voter in the

United States is considerably less than in Venezuela, the Federal Republic of Germany, Israel, and Ireland for comparable elections. The cost in Canada is higher than in America, if the value of free television and radio are included. Because of the absence of data, it is not easy to know how United Kingdom costs compare to ours.

In preparing this essay it was striking to find that in most of the twenty countries with 1.5 million voters and twenty-five years of continuous democratic practice, there is neither adequate financing data nor recognized experts with the knowledge and experience to make informed and generally accepted judgments of costs. Nearly half of the countries require *no* reports from parties or candidates. Half of the remainder have laws requiring limited information, or enforce their laws so casually that the reports are incomplete, implausible, or both.

Under these circumstances, any inclusive assertions that electoral campaigns are conducted at a much lower cost in all other democracies are made without sufficient data or by using criteria that are clearly inadequate. If the six countries whose expenditures were examined here are indicative, it is probable that the per eligible voter costs are less in the United States than in most other democracies.

Howard Penniman *is an AEI resident scholar.*

PART FOUR

Messages about the Media

by Michael Jay Robinson and Maura Clancey

Teflon Politics

Ron Nessen likes to say that if it didn't happen on the evening news, then it didn't happen. He should know; Nessen is the only person ever to work from both sides—as a network correspondent and as a presidential press secretary. But what Nessen neglects to say is that even if it *did* happen on the evening news, it still might not have "happened," at least as far as the public is concerned.

We have just completed a national, scientific phone survey of 366 adult Americans (April 14-16), and we are convinced that news coverage—even time on network television—doesn't translate directly into celebrity status or into public awareness. In our poll, whether the question involved Ed Meese's cronies or Gary Hart's original surname, the public enthusiastically exhibited its right *not* to know.

To the Best of Their Recollection

The first item on our questionnaire tapped the public memory about the year's top stories. "Over the last twelve months," we asked, "which news event would you say you remember the most?" We offered no hints.

Questions like this scare people, and about half the respondents who hung up on us during the survey did so after hearing this one. Even those respondents brave enough to continue remembered little about current events, nor did they equate news with political news.

A large proportion of our subjects balked at the idea of remembering a major event—and if they did, we asked them the same question again, giving them as much time as they needed to come up with something—anything. Even so, about one-fourth (23 percent) of our sample could recall nothing in the news from the last twelve months. In fact, the single most memorable news event for the last year turned out to be "can't remember" (see table 1).

Many of those who could recall something came up with events that had taken place two or more years ago—the war in the Falklands, the Tylenol scare, and

Brezhnev's death, to name a few. Another fifth of the sample offered nonpolitical events—the sorts of things no self-respecting journalist would consider "real" news: volcano eruptions, weather reports, accidents, and sports news. All told, over 40 percent of our sample mentioned "nothing" or nonpolitical events as what they remembered most in 1983-1984.

To be fair, six of the ten most memorable stories were political (table 1). Nonetheless, our figures suggest the public remembers hard news the way Ronald Reagan remembers hard facts—fitfully, at best. They also suggest that news audiences have at least as great an interest in the mundane as the political. Criminal acts were precisely as memorable as *everything* going on in Central America. Soviet leader Yuri Andropov's death barely surpassed the death of rock/gospel singer Marvin Gaye as the year's most memorable obituary (Andropov having suffered the twin misfortunes of dying outside a major media center and of natural causes, not murder).

Murders and murderers totally outdistanced foreign wars or foreign anything. For example, homicidal maniacs, as a class, proved seven times as memorable as the brutal war between Iran and Iraq.

But it isn't just homespun violence that outdoes

Table 1

TOP TEN MOST MEMORABLE NEWS EVENTS
IN THE LAST 12 MONTHS

Can't remember	23%
Beirut bombing	14
Campaign/Elections, general	12
Grenada invasion	7
Space shuttle	6
Marine pullout	4
KAL Flight 007	3
Weather	3
Lebanese war	2
Christopher Wilder	2
Hart campaign	2

politics or foreign affairs—news recollections are about as pedestrian as they are prurient or provincial. In what might be the most memorable finding about less-than-memorable news, the Soviet attack on Flight 007 proved no more newsworthy in the public's collective memory than the year's weather. In fact, the Korean jet massacre—so big in the media—proved only half as salient to the public as news about the U.S. space shuttle program.

These numbers reflect a public far less political than politicians or journalists usually assume, and a public possessing an astoundingly short memory. People recall the politics of yesterday, not the day before. Only four months after Jesse Jackson's stunning success in bringing Lt. Robert Goodman back from his Syrian captivity, for example, a miniscule 1 percent of the public was able to list that series of events among the most memorable. Christopher Wilder, race-car driver turned killer, does "better" than Jackson's rescue mission in refreshing memories because, in part, Wilder made news in April, not in January.

We found public memory about news and world affairs short enough to qualify as mass amnesia. In fact, the thesis that Americans are, more than most, willing to forgive and forget may have less to do with the former than with their astounding capacity for the latter.

Ed Meese and Charles "The Killer" Wick

A week before we conducted our survey, Louis Harris presented America with national polling data that showed the public had decided Attorney General-designate Ed Meese had to go. Our survey indicates that the same public barely knows that Ed Meese was ever here.

We asked our respondents, "Have you heard the name Ed Meese?" One-quarter of the sample said "No." We then asked those who had heard Meese's name why he had been in the news lately. One-quarter

of them had to admit they couldn't remember anything at all about Meese, or they told us things that weren't true. ("His recent tragic death" was a shocking example of misinformation.)

Another 10 percent could recall only that Meese had recently been designated as attorney general. Two percent of our respondents said Meese was about to be made secretary of state, which, we concluded, was either misinformation or a hot tip. And murder being much on the minds of our sample, one woman claimed that Ed Meese was a vicious killer—something not even Senator Howard Metzenbaum has intimated.

About a third (36 percent) of the entire sample did link Ed Meese to financial problems, his indiscretion concerning loans, cuff-links, cronyism, or his insensitivity toward hunger in America.

So how did Louis Harris get these people to volunteer an opinion about someone they didn't recognize? Quite simply, he never asked them whether they knew Meese or not. And, by describing his version of what Meese had done before asking for opinions, Harris could be fairly certain that people would have something to say.

Harris's respondents were faced with the following *lead* item—one that was quintessentially Harris in style: "Agree or disagree: Since federal law says that high officials must report all loans they receive, it looks as though Meese violated the law by not reporting a $15,000 loan from a couple who were close friends, both of whom later got federal jobs paying a combined total of close to $100,000 a year." (77 percent agreed, 15 percent disagreed, 8 percent were not sure.)

Looking at the question, we're not surprised at the results. But the real issue isn't so much Harris's methodology as it is the level of knowledge the public possesses about Attorney General-designate Edwin Meese. After all, it makes little sense to argue that Americans want dismissed from office a man about whom they

know nothing.

Perhaps Harris felt safe in assuming people knew Ed Meese. After all, he had dominated a fair share of the news for several weeks. We checked abstracts of the evening news programs for the month of March—the month in which Meese's problems really began. Meese made the network news forty-three times in just thirty-one days, and he was the lead story on eight separate occasions—total news time: 5,100 seconds. But despite Meese's ongoing status as a lead story on network news during the month before our survey, the Meese mess, no matter how generously defined, failed to penetrate the cognitive map of even four Americans out of ten.

Nonetheless, when compared to Charles Z. Wick, problem-plagued director of the USIA, Ed Meese is a celebrity. Wick's case magnifies everything said so far about levels of public information, extensiveness of news coverage, and the tenuousness of the relationship between the two.

Let's be fair. Since the beginning of the year Charles Wick has received only a fraction of the news coverage that Ed Meese has attracted. Still, back in January when Wick was a hot news story, network evening news featured him no fewer than ten times—five times as often as the networks featured Gary Hart during the same four-week period. Ten bad news reports in a month—half of them presented before the first commercial—puts the Wick affair somewhere between a major media story and an inside-the-Beltway press flap.

The facts in the Wick case were anything but trivial. Having lied to the *New York Times*, having slurred Margaret Thatcher and her sex, having secretly taped phone calls with Jimmy Carter and dozens of other private citizens—all in a year's time—Wick might well have become a household word in a world populated with the politically interested. Yet, in our survey three-quarters of the public had never heard his name! A microscopic *2 percent* of our sample could tell us anything at all accurate about Wick—good, bad, or indifferent. In fact, because Wick was, at the time of our poll, unlucky enough to own the same initials as Christopher Wilder, he was about as likely to be identified as a mass murderer as he was to be linked directly to his secret taping enterprise.

The Economy—What Recovery?

Our initial hunch was that the public would know more about the economy than about recent political scandals. We were right, but barely. Even on basic questions involving unemployment, the public knew only a little more than random responses would predict.

We asked each respondent the following question about the employment picture: "Would you say that *over the last six months* the unemployment rate has gotten worse, leveled off, or gotten better?" Despite the real and dramatic drop in unemployment rates over the last eighteen months, less than half (44 percent) of the respondents chose the right answer—"gotten better." Twenty percent actually said the unemployment rate had "gotten worse." Given that every respondent was provided with three clear choices, chance alone should have netted correct answers from a third of the sample.

The public did even worse on the inflation question. We asked whether *"during the Reagan years* the inflation rate has gotten worse, leveled off, or gotten better?" Just over 60 percent answered this one wrong, saying that the rate had gotten worse or leveled off during Reagan's term. Again, since this was a three-part multiple choice question, one would estimate that a third of the sample would have guessed right by chance alone. The public did only 6 percent better at getting the right answer than probability would allow.

There are several interpretations for these mistaken notions about the economy. First, one could point to the trickiness of the questions, hence the problematic nature of the right answers. For example, the rate of inflation is way down since Reagan took office, but prices are, of course, higher than they were under Carter. Next, one could blame the media for having given so little attention to inflation rates once they abated, and so much attention to unemployment rates once they took off. That's not a bad interpretation, and some of this confusion about the recovery can be linked to the news bias in favor of hyping economic failures and ignoring economic successes. But that bias won't explain why the same public couldn't tell us much about Ed Meese or anything at all about Charles Wick—two topics the media did not, to say the least, play down in 1984. The facts about the economy seem almost as unriveting in the American psyche as the facts about scandals in the Reagan administration.

Campaign '84—Primary Education

At one point in 1984—the ten days between the Maine caucuses and Super Tuesday—pollsters estimate that Gary Hart was picking up three million (!) supporters per day in his quest for the Democratic nomination. At some point people were learning something—at the very least that Gary Hart was alive if not well, and that he was *not* Walter Mondale. In fact, our poll also picked up on some of this.

One set of questions did produce correct answers that went way beyond statistical chance—questions about primaries. As late as April 15—more than six weeks after the fact—over half (55 percent) of our sample knew that Gary Hart had won the New Hampshire primary. Even though 45 percent guessed wrong or didn't know who had won, public awareness of Hart's victory proves that the facts about the New Hampshire primary registered.

Nor is it just the New Hampshire primary that jogs their minds. Practically two-thirds (65 percent) knew (without prompting) that Walter Mondale had won the week's big primary in Pennsylvania. The media, then, do provide a "primary education" in an election year. Our people knew more about winners and losers in primaries than they knew about anything else. No doubt, the behavior of the news media themselves explains a good deal of this—horse-race journalism in the news produces horse race sensitivity in the public. But, again, news focus doesn't explain fully why winners and losers stick better in the national memory than other day-to-day news events.

Hartpence, Schmartpence

What makes public knowledge of primary winners even more intriguing is that it does not extend to the major campaign issues of the day. Ever since Hart's coup in New Hampshire, for example, all the news media have given big play to Gary Hart's alias: Gary Hart, a.k.a. Gary Hartpence.

The "Hartpence" story represents the second greatest press/campaign issue since the Iowa caucuses —superseded only by the "Hymie" affair, news coverage of Jesse Jackson's public relations wars with the Jewish community. Hart's decision to undergo a formal name-change operation during law school, and his subsequent decision to blame his dead father for the idea, have been near the top of the list of stories about Hart the man and Hart the candidate.

Yet we found that almost two-thirds (64 percent) of our sample neither knew nor could guess which Democrat had received attention for having changed his name—even though by mid-April there were only three Democrats left in the race. Roger Mudd's infamous interview with Senator Hart notwithstanding, the percentage of people actually knowing that Hart had changed his name was, in a three-man field, ever-so-slightly better than a third.

And the Winner Is . . . Wendy's

The Hartpence issue has not, to this point, penetrated very deeply into the electoral consciousness. And, to his credit, Walter Mondale never made much of Hart's original name, or its transformation.

Instead Mondale fought Hart with a campaign slogan from America's fast-food wars. Having done so, Mondale did himself some good, and gave us some insight into the kind of news that does pierce the shield of public indifference.

Throughout March and April, Walter Mondale and the campaign press corps repeated the question "Where's the Beef?", a much less than subtle slam against Gary Hart's new-ideas campaign. And, as it turned out, the public learned more about this silly slogan than it learned about some of the more serious campaign issues of the year.

Without prompting, 44 percent of our respondents could tell us "what slogan from a popular TV commercial Walter Mondale had used to criticize Gary Hart," and a whopping 88 percent of those people could iden-

tify the company that had originated the commercial— Wendy's, of course.

Let's put that set of figures in perspective. A slightly larger percentage of our sample could tell us about "Where's the Beef" than could tell us which way inflation had gone under Reagan. The percentage able to cite the Wendy's ad (without multiple choices) was equal to the percentage who could tell us which way the year's unemployment rate was headed (with choices). All this is, of course, terrible news for Reagan fans— and not much better for fans of democratic theory. Wendy's, however, should be delighted.

The Teflon Candidate

Phrase-making counts in politics as well as commercials. And when Pat Schroeder (D.-Col.) retires from the House of Representatives, she may well be remembered most for the phrase she invented to describe Ronald Reagan—the Teflon candidate, the politician to whom bad news never seems to stick. Richard Cohen, *Washington Post* columnist, simply refers to Reagan as "The Great Rondini."

One of the original reasons for conducting this survey was to gauge the thickness of Reagan's Teflon coating. So we asked three questions about Reagan and his administration that might tap the extent to which the Great Rondini can escape the bad press he or his administration receives.

Let's start with church attendance. For months the Democrats had been complaining about Reagan's miserable record at Sunday services. When the school prayer amendment reached the Senate floor (in March), the Democrats made an issue of Reagan's church-going. The White House had to release an embarrassing statement admitting that the president had not formally visited a church since last June—not for nine months.

Though never a major story, the press release and the Democratic charges about Reagan's hypocrisies, did make news in March and April. And, with the facts admitted by the White House, we had a tailor-made case for testing Reagan's Teflon shield. We asked the following item: "Would you say that Mr. Reagan himself attends church services outside of the White House almost every week, two or three times a month, about once a month, less than once a month?"

Thirty percent knew the right answer—either that Reagan goes to church less than once a month or that he hadn't been to church since last spring. But 70 percent didn't know (55 percent) or refused to answer (15 percent). Reagan had a much better churchgoer image than either the facts or his press coverage could possibly justify. Some respondents told us that Reagan must go to church every week, given the way he talks about prayer.

Another pair of questions implies that Ronald Reagan does have a nonstick surface. We asked identical questions about Reagan's ethical principles and those of his staff. Specifically, we asked whether "Reagan is

Table 2
LIKELIHOOD OF FOLLOWING "STRICT ETHICAL PRINCIPLES"

	Ronald Reagan	Members of Reagan administration
Almost all the time	15%	6%
Most of the time	40	29
Some of the time	27	46
Rarely	14	11
Refused	4	7

a man who follows strict ethical principles almost all of the time, most of the time, some of the time, or rarely?" Then we asked the same question about the people who work in the Reagan administration.

As table 2 indicates, Reagan runs well ahead of his staff—twenty points ahead if one considers the first two choices ("almost all of the time" and "most of the time") as the positive response. Still, slightly over 40 percent of our sample chose the negative responses; they consider him less than committed to strict ethical principles.

Apparently, Ronald Reagan is only stick-resistant, not stick-proof—not so much Teflon II as Teflon I, with scratches. Nevertheless, his image is better than that of his administration.

Conclusions

The first conclusion is the least original—the public knows less about politics than journalists or politicians think they know.

The second conclusion derives from the first. For the mass audience, news is not necessarily politics. Violent crimes are more memorable as news events than all but the most dramatic political occurrences. Rupert Murdoch has a much better grasp of news audiences than do his detractors.

The third conclusion is slightly less elitist. We also recognize that it isn't simply the mass public that pays so little attention to what's happening in current events. The case of Ronald Reagan is vintage, but so is the more vivid case of Congressman Ed Markey (D.-Mass.), until recently a candidate for the United States Senate. Two months ago on a Boston talk show, Markey was asked to name the prime minister of Israel. Markey admitted he didn't know, then guessed wrong.

Perhaps even more startling is that—as of early May—only two of the three Democratic contestants for president knew much about Louis Farrakhan and his threats against reporters or Jews who criticize Jesse Jackson. In the Texas TV debate on May 2, Gary Hart had to admit that he was mostly in the dark about the ongoing battle between Farrakhan and the news reporter he had threatened with death back in March. A *Newsweek* poll conducted the last week in April indicates that only about half the public knows about Louis Farrakhan or anything concerning Jesse Jackson's alleged anti-Semitic remarks.

So political leaders do better, but not all that much better than the mass public when it comes to hard facts. Looking at our own survey qualitatively, the results suggest that Eric Sevareid probably has the best overall interpretation of public awareness: Never overestimate their level of information—never underestimate their ability to reason. Our respondents didn't know many answers, but they did seem to know how to think about facts they did possess.

Fourth, polls that tap sentiments about politicians who are virtually unknown to the public ought not to be taken very seriously, or not to be taken at all. What might be more useful is to tap sentiments about something that people do have feelings about—pollsters. For example, why not the following item? "Agree or disagree: When a national pollster asks questions about a politician's problems, knowing that most Americans don't know who that politician is, that pollster may have problems of his own."

Fifth, the news media have some, but by no means total, say in setting the agenda, or controlling what the public learns. Events are just like politicians—some stick better than others in public consciousness, for reasons we don't always understand.

Sixth, slogans seem to work better than abstractions, or even personalities, in penetrating public indifference. News coverage of "Where's the Beef?" and Wendy's did much better at puncturing national consciousness than did coverage of Ed Meese or Gary Hartpence. Apparently the public retains very little from the political messages they receive. Even more dismaying is the distinct possibility that phrasemaking represents the single best strategy in promoting a candidate, an issue, or a theme.

Finally, there is something to the Teflon nature of Ronald Reagan. Reagan runs well ahead of his press and his political advisers. But that fact ought not to detract from the larger truth—that politics is itself Teflon coated. Good news or bad, political messages of all types usually fail to reach their target in any efficient way. And those messages and those news items that do penetrate usually fall out of public consciousness within a few days or weeks. Ronald Reagan has a nonstick surface, but he's not alone. Almost nothing sticks easily or for very long. Politics comes treated with a Teflon coating of its own. ☑

The authors wish to thank John P. Robinson, Robert Feuerherd, Lisa Grand, Robert Heilferty, and Maryanne Wynne for their help in conducting the survey.

Michael Jay Robinson *is a visiting scholar at AEI and director of the Media Analysis Project at George Washington University.*

Maura Clancey *is a provost fellow in the Arts and Humanities Division of the University of Maryland.*

by David R. Gergen

The Message to the Media

During the furor over the government's treatment of the press in Grenada last fall, sharply different views emerged about American regard for the fourth estate:

"Dr. Gloom": Many commentators, deluged with critical calls and mail, decided that the public was finally fed up with the press. *Time* magazine devoted an extraordinary cover story to the subject of "Journalism Under Fire," and said the dispute over Grenada "seemed to uncork a pent-up hostility." Public respect for journalism, said the editors, "has fallen dramatically in recent years, threatening one of the foundations of the country's democratic system."

"Dr. Pangloss": Hold on, cried Louis Harris, rushing in with a freshly minted poll showing that a majority thought the press should have accompanied the troops into Grenada. The darker conclusions are not only wrong, said Harris, but reflect "panic" and a "deep sense of insecurity in the media," which have "a real lack of understanding and faith in the public's ability to appreciate what a free press is all about."

Well, which view is correct? Judging from a mound of research materials covering nearly a half century and collected by the editors of *Public Opinion*, the answer seems to be . . . neither. It's far more complex.

Here are the principal conclusions that can be drawn from available research:

• A majority of Americans do harbor heartfelt reservations and even resentments about the press, but these feelings are certainly not new. They have come to the surface with increasing frequency since the dawn of the television age.

• Apparently, a major source of the problem is the public's diminishing faith in the accuracy and fairness of the press and a widespread view that the press emphasizes too much bad news.

• Yet, even as its credibility has slipped, the press is still respected relative to other institutions. The public believes that the press is contributing more to the "public good" than government, business, or labor. And, if forced to choose, the public will tend to put more credence in a story from a journalist than one from a high-ranking government official.

• Local newspapers and television stations receive higher marks from the public than the national press, both for the quality of reporting and contributions to the public good.

• All things considered, the public wants a vigorous free press and supports the basic tenets of the First Amendment. Just as its views of the press are mixed, however, the public is warier than the Supreme Court about supporting the outer reaches of the First Amendment, and it is decidedly more eager to suppress and censor when matters of public morality or national security are at stake.

Bubbling Resentment

While many analysts lately have recalled how often the press was criticized during its partisan, brawling days in the early 19th century and later on during the era of "yellow journalism," few have remembered more recent history. Long before Grenada, it was apparent that just beneath the surface in modern America run deep currents of resentment toward the press.

Dwight Eisenhower drew them out in a memorable moment at the 1964 Republican convention when he pointed toward the press gallery and urged delegates to ignore "sensation-seeking columnists and commentators, because, my friends, I assure you that these are people who couldn't care less about the good of our party." As described by correspondent Jim Deakin: "Reporters who were there . . . will forget the scene that ensued about the same time they forget Adolph Hitler. The convention exploded in a pandemonium or rage against the news media. The delegates stood on their chairs, shouting, raving, shaking their fists, and cursing the reporters in the press section."

Six years later, when Spiro Agnew leveled his blasts against the "nattering nabobs of negativism," 56 percent told Louis Harris that Agnew was right. In March 1970, CBS found that advocates of freedom of the press were only 42 percent of its sample.

During the decade that followed, ill feelings about the press showed up not only in libel suits and Hollywood movies, but also in a number of opinion polls. The most widely quoted survey numbers— to which we shall return—were the measurements of public confidence in institutions that Harris began taking in 1966. The number expressing "high" confidence in the press fell from 29 percent in 1966 to a low of 14 percent in 1982 (it rose to 19 percent in 1983). By 1981, a plurality of Americans were telling the *Los Angeles Times* they perceived a left-of-center tilt in national television, and in 1983, by a margin of 52-42, a small sample of respondents (501 interviewed) told ABC News that "the news media are too powerful."

The Public Indictment

While most other major institutions have also suffered a decline in public confidence in recent years, the erosion of confidence in the press seems at least partly rooted in phenomena that are unique to journalism— and thus a source of concern to many editors and executives today.

One of the most damaging changes that has occurred has been the decline of belief in press accuracy, long a foundation of its credibility. In 1939, Elmo Roper found that 68 percent of those he surveyed said news stories in the papers were "always" or "usually" accurate. In 1958, 70 percent vouched for newspaper accuracy to George Gallup. Contrast those results with opinions registered in a survey conducted in December 1983 and January 1984 by Clark, Martire & Bartholomeo for the American Society of Newspaper Editors (ASNE): By 48 to 41 percent, Americans now reject the idea that newspaper stories are "usually accurate and almost always get their facts straight"; by 48 to 43 percent, they also turn thumbs down on the accuracy of television. Editors today often worry that too many readers personally involved with stories lose faith because they discover distortions or errors. As if to confirm that suspicion, almost one-third of those surveyed told the *Los Angeles Times* in 1981 that the media were usually inaccurate in reporting news they knew about personally.

Along with assertions about inaccuracies have come growing concerns about *fairness* and *bias* in the press. While surveys in the 1930s and 40s sometimes revealed feelings that the press had been one-sided in political coverage (favoring the GOP over FDR) the general perception was one of balance. In 1937, for example, here's what Roper found:

Is the press fair?

Yes 66%

No 27

But something dramatic has happened since then. This is what Ruth Clark found in 1984:

Newspapers are usually fair; they bend over backward to tell both sides of the story.

Agree 38%

Disagree 50 (!)

Television stories are usually fair; they bend over backward to tell both sides of the story.

Agree 29%

Disagree 63 (!!)

The news is not all bad for the media. A 1982 study by Bud Roper for the Television Information Office found that in assessing the way TV treats different groups— clergy, blue-collar workers, women, and others—a consensus thought that every group was treated fairly. Only blacks were likely to think that they were being less fairly treated than the rest of the population. (The resentments of blacks and other minorities toward their portrayal in the press may well be a driving force behind the nation's changing attitudes toward the media; available research does not permit an adequate answer.)

In her presentation to the newspaper editors, Ruth Clark, president of Clark, Martire & Bartholomeo, pointed out that "fairness" covers a wide range of readers' concerns. Among them, she said, are the beliefs that: there is too much editorializing in news columns, and too little effort to get at all the facts (55 percent told ABC News in 1983 that print reporters give too many of their own opinions and not enough facts); newspapers fail to cover inadequate services in poor areas; they treat the rich better than the poor; and they offer inadequate coverage of particular neighborhoods. "Crime in the rich neighborhoods is sexy and good gossip," said one respondent. "In my area, it's violent and ugly."

Bad News and Biased News

Interwoven with the question of balance is the question of bias, or how slanted coverage is. The press has long had a problem here. In the 1930s, both Gallup and Roper found majorities believed newspapers left out or soft-pedaled stories that were important to advertisers. In her 1984 study for ASNE, Clark found that once again, a majority (57 percent) thought that news coverage in newspapers is often influenced by advertisers and other business interests.

Yankelovich, Skelly and White have suggested that the public's definition of bias may have changed since the 1930s. Their surveys in the 1970s found 72 percent thought TV and newspapers probably slanted news and distorted events, and 7 out of 10 also defined bias as "putting too much emphasis on bad news and not the good."

The complaint about too much bad news is recurrent, but it is being pressed with new forcefulness today as a series of new media studies appear. One scholar in the field, Michael Robinson, learned from monitoring national television that the networks are innocent of the charge that they are too liberal in their news, but they should be indicted for rampant negativism. Apparently, the public strongly agrees. Consider this 1983 question by the ABC News/*Washington Post* survey team:

Do you think TV news concentrates too much on bad news and not enough on good news?

Yes 73%

No 22

Ruth Clark, who also found large majorities saying there was too much bad news in newspapers and television (the numbers modestly declined between 1979 and 1984) reported to ASNE this spring that blacks, minorities, and the less educated are particularly inclined toward this criticism.

In 1980 the Public Agenda Foundation, founded by Daniel Yankelovich, took a look at a number of press issues and concluded that many Americans use "bad news" as a catch-all phrase. They see it not only as frequent reporting of disturbing events, but also as the presence of hype, sensationalism, and questionable news judgment. Large majorities told Clark's interviewers this year that both television and newspapers sensationalize news to make it more interesting.

The bottom line for the press, when all these charges are added up, is the question of *credibility*. Unfortunately, we know very little about press credibility in the 1930s and 1940s. We do know, however, that in 1981 only 3 in 10 told George Gallup that they believed "most" of what they heard and read in the news media; 5 out of 10 said they believed only "some" of the news.

Television news, as has been widely reported, is regarded as more credible than newspapers, just as radio news was often seen as more credible than the papers in the 1940s. A regular series of surveys by the Roper Organization for the Television Information Office found that TV news began to surpass the newspapers as a credible source in 1961 and has steadily widened its lead: In 1982, TV beat the newspapers by 53 to 22 percent on which medium was the more credible.

Strengths of the Press

Lest the public indictment of the press be exaggerated, it is important to acknowledge that the press also has several recognized strengths, especially compared to other institutions.

Let's return to the polls measuring public confidence. In their book, *The Confidence Gap*, Seymour

Martin Lipset and William Schneider point out that during the 1970s, a "see-saw" relationship seemed to develop between the executive branch and the press. Drawing upon Harris and National Opinion Research Center (NORC) studies, they show that during the Watergate period, confidence in the executive branch dropped from 26 to 15 percent, while confidence in the press rose from 20 to 28 percent. President Carter's early days brought a resurgence of respect for the executive (and a drop for the press), but as regard for him diminished, trust in the press increased. The data seem to suggest that when the government is not performing well, the public welcomes the watchdog role that the press can play. (In 1983, interestingly, both the press and the executive enjoyed an increase in public trust.)

One of the most comprehensive reviews of public attitudes toward the press, written in *Presstime* magazine last year by Maxwell E. McCombs and Laura Washington, makes another pertinent point: While overall confidence in the press has declined since the late 1960s, other social institutions have fallen more steeply. "High" levels of confidence in the press dropped by about a third by 1983; education, Congress, major companies, and labor dropped by well over half. It is also true that by some measures, trust in the press has been much more stable than some imagine. Gallup, for example, asks people whether they have a "great deal, quite a lot, some, or very little" confidence in various institutions. In 1973, 39 percent said they had a "great deal" or "quite a lot" of confidence in the press; in 1983, 38 percent answered that way—essentially no change over the decade.

More to the point, when the public is asked to make comparisons between institutions as opposed to evaluating the media by itself, some striking views emerge. Consider this battery of questions that the *Los Angeles Times* posed to a nationwide sample in 1981:

Institutions with the highest standards of honesty and integrity:

Media	36%
Business	17
Government	16
Labor	12

Institution that has done the most to promote the "public good":

Media	36%
Business	17
Government	17
Labor	16

Institution that should have its power cut back for the good of the country:

Government	35%
Labor	21
Business	14
Media	12

As if that weren't difficult enough to swallow for government officials who enjoy flailing the press, there are some other numbers that say the spokesmen of the media have greater credibility than those who take issue with them. In 1983, the *Los Angeles Times* asked how often government, television, and newspapers give out biased information. The answers were the same for all three: a little better than 4 in 10 said each institution "often" or "always" gives out bum dope. In 1983, ABC News asked a small sample whom they believe when high government officials deny reports in the press. Their findings: high officials—32 percent, national news media—47 percent (!!!).

Moreover, the public seems to like the more aggressive reporting of today. Some 79 percent told Gallup in 1981 that they approve of investigative reporting, and 66 percent said they would like to see more of it. But certain newsgathering techniques draw fire. For example, two-thirds say reporters should identify themselves, and half object to running stories quoting unnamed sources. There is also widespread opposition to television invading the privacy of ordinary citizens.

When passing out plaudits to the press, Americans reserve the most enthusiastic for *local* newspapers and television stations. The polls have good news for both. Ruth Clark's 1984 study for ASNE, for example, shows that while a majority feel the national papers are unfair, less than 40 percent say the same about their own local newspaper. Over eight in ten also say their local newspaper cares about their community, is useful and is accurate. Similarly, studies done for the television industry by the Roper Organization find that local TV stations are well regarded. Fully seven in ten said their local television station is doing an "excellent" or "good" job in 1982—the highest number saying that for any local institution. Careful readers of opinion polls will recognize a familiar pattern here: citizens tend to have a higher regard for their own congressman or newspaper than for the Congress or the national press.

Some Fences Around a Free Press

Where does this congeries of feelings leave the public on the core concern of the press: the First Amendment?

Clearly, there are not only mixed feelings, but also genuine confusion. In 1980, over seven out of ten told Gallup they did not know what the amendment was or does. The Pentagon Papers case made that point, too. While a preponderance of people then supported the right of the *New York Times* to publish, there was great uncertainty about ground rules. A plurality wanted to be told the truth about Vietnam, but 70 percent thought the documents should not be published "if there is any doubt about violating national security."

On clear-cut, down-the-middle issues of the First Amendment, the public seems to side with a free press. Some 84 percent told Ruth Clark this year that they would be "upset enough to do something" if the government tried to shut down a newspaper, and only 25 percent—down from 42 percent in 1979—said the pres-

ident has a right to stop a newspaper from printing a story he feels is biased or inaccurate. A 1981 survey by the *Los Angeles Times* found that by a 53-39 percent margin, Americans thought the press did not abuse its privileges under the First Amendment, and of those who felt differently, only one in five thought the government ought to correct the abuse through regulation.

Yet, as Herbert McClosky and Alida Brill underscore in their new book *Dimensions of Tolerance* the general public has not yet come to accept the broadest interpretations of the First Amendment made by the Supreme Court. Based on their own surveys, the authors make a strong case that in two particular areas—public morality and national security—the public is much less dedicated to civil liberties than are community leaders and the "legal elite." By 46 to 36 percent, for instance, the public endorses a federal board of television censors to protect against violent or obscene shows; community leaders reject the board by 45 to 36 percent, and the "legal elite" reject it, 55 to 27.

Survey after survey has also shown a special public sensitivity to publication of news stories that might damage national security. In 1983, ABC News found that by a 2 to 1 margin, people agreed that the federal government should be allowed to censor news stories before they appear "if the government feels national security might be endangered by the story."

These conflicting feelings left the public in a quandary during the Grenada invasion—a quandary that also showed up in public polls. Louis Harris, as noted earlier, found the public opposed to the government's temporary ban on live press coverage: so did a survey by ABC News and the *Washington Post*. But polls by the *Los Angeles Times* and Roper, taken at approximately the same time, came out the other way. There was only one point of agreement: All polls showed that the public would like the press to be included in future military exercises—unless that would endanger national security. Back to square one.

* * *

A review of public surveys, then, lends little credence to the view that in late 1983, the American people suddenly rose up in wrath, ready to crush the freedom and arrogance of the press for its many sins. Still less, however, does it support the rosy picture of a public that retains complete faith and confidence in the press. The American people have come to depend heavily upon the press, and they welcome its mission, but they are also sending some warning signals.

Incidentally, there was one more signal that came from the Ruth Clark study. A majority of readers told her that one of the most aggravating things about newspapers is the way ink comes off on your hands. Now *there's* a cover story! ☑

David Gergen *is an AEI visiting fellow in communications and a fellow at Harvard's Institute of Politics.*

by Edwin Diamond

New Wrinkles on the Permanent Press

What a difference a decade makes. Ten years ago this summer the holder of the highest office in the land was brought low by two intrepid—and unknown—reporters from the *Washington Post*. In the popular iconography of the press, the Republic was saved by the white hats, Woodward and Bernstein, and by the all-recording eye of television news.

Cut to 1984. Now it is the press that is being brought low in the public esteem. Woodstein has given way to the Sally Field character in *Absence of Malice*, who sacrifices a life on the altar of her big story. A recent Gallup poll reports that almost half the American public approved of the way the Reagan administration kept the press out of Grenada—and a lot more people wonder why that awful Sam Donaldson is being so disrespectful to our amiable president. Now, the journalists wear the black hats, or at least the sweaty hatbands.

In truth, both popular pictures of then and now are out of focus. The *Washington Post*'s Watergate coverage was hardly typical of the year's journalism, much less of an institution as diverse as the American press. Three separate surveys done at the time, including one by our News Study Group at MIT, reveal how little press attention Watergate attracted outside the *Washington Post* in the period from the June break-in to the November election. Similarly, in 1984, public opinion ratings of the press are drifting downward to the level of auto salesmen and psychologists, even as the three networks' share of the television audience is steadily eroding; but we are still a long way from the day when people stop watching Dan Rather, or when they turn out the lights at CBS News or any of the other major media organizations. The big boys and girls of the 1970s are brawnier today than ever before.

Nevertheless, what actually has been happening to the established news organizations of the United States over the past ten years makes for a better, more provocative story than what you may have been hearing in the media. But then isn't that usually the case? They hardly ever tell us the real news.

If we comb out our prejudices, knee-jerk responses, and wishful thinking and concentrate on the hard data, these are the four relevant headlines about the media in America today:

1. The news industry has never been economically healthier: The rich have been getting richer.
The business of America being business, almost all the vital economic signs are good, medium by medium. There are, it's true, fewer daily papers today than in 1974—1,710 compared to 1,768 a decade ago; but daily circulation at 62.4 million copies today is higher than in 1974. At the same time, advertising gains, coupled with the conversion to new electronic technology, have produced profit percentages for newspaper companies that nearly double the average for the Fortune 500 corporations. A typical, established media conglomerate like the *New York Times* Company, for example, just gave its shareholders a three-for-one stock split and then rewarded them with a record rise of 24 percent in income for the first quarter of 1984 from its newspaper, magazine, and broadcast groups.

Among magazines, circulation and profits have reached record highs. More magazines are published today, and more people are reading them—perhaps as many as 20 percent more readers today than in the mid-1970s, according to figures from the Magazine Publishers Association. More to the point, the three established news weeklies, *Time*, *Newsweek*, and *U.S. News & World Report*, have gradually increased readership in the last few years after a period of somewhat stagnant circulation in the 1970s. Based on marketing studies of so-called pass-along readers, the three news weeklies together command an audience of perhaps 50 million a week—practically speaking, a sweep of the educated, news-consuming public.

What makes these readership figures so impressive is that this audience has been assembled in the face of increasing competition for the consumer's attention from television. Earlier this year, for example, the Television Advertising Bureau reported that TV viewing in the average American household surpassed seven hours a day for the first time. This means that the average household set is on seven hours, though individual household members may spend on the average no more than two or two and one-half hours each day watching. Not only is there more TV watching; there is also more news and informational programming to watch. The network news programs once were loss leaders; the ad dollars from "I Love Lucy" used to pay for Walter Cronkite, the industry was fond of saying. Today, "Sixty Minutes" and Dan Rather earn millions for "Cagney and Lacey."

2. Challenges to the established media have not been successful—so far.

The major print development of the 1980s has been the start-up of Gannett's *USA Today*, which calls itself, rather grandly, "the nation's newspaper." In fact, *USA Today*, with its colorful graphics and departmental approach to the news, is as much a daily news magazine as a newspaper. Visually, *USA Today* has shaken up the ponderous habits of the newspaper industry; dozens of newspapers added splashes of color to their pages after Gannett showed how it could be done. But *USA Today* has not gained advertising acceptance to go with its breathtaking circulation rises. Current readership is around 1.3 million after less than two years of publication, but the advertising pages that are the key to profitability have lagged at six pages a day, on the average, and the paper needs to stop the flow of red ink that topped $110 million in 1983. While there are compelling economic reasons why advertisers have stayed away from *USA Today*—its cpm, or cost per thousand, is not much different from that of *U.S. News*, and the news weekly has a longer shelf life—there are also editorial reasons. *USA Today* has been so determined to be short and snappy, with no news story longer than a few paragraphs, that it has achieved a bland, fast-food taste—McPaper. It has gained the reputation as a paper for people who don't like to read papers.

Light readers and nonreaders usually find their way to television. And in the last decade, too, cable and other news media have emerged to challenge the long-standing triopoly of the traditional networks. As with the major print outlets, ABC, CBS, and NBC continue to enjoy healthy profits, even as their share of market declines. In 1978, the combined three-network share of homes watching prime-time television was 94 percent. By 1981, this figure had fallen to 84 percent, and it has continued dropping in 1984, with occasional contrary blips. Research studies by the J. Walter Thompson agency and others confirm this trend and predict a further sharp drop to the range of 60-65 percent by 1990. These are not "lost" viewers; they show up at the offerings for sports, movies, and specials on cable and on pay TV.

The network news and information programs have been relatively insulated from these shocks. Indeed, the competition between the traditional news organizations and the upstart cable companies has been one-sided so far. The Satellite News Channel faltered, and only Ted Turner's Cable News Network is close to breaking even. New media enterprises have failed so far to win bigger audiences for a simple reason. People who market a new service, as the telecommunications writer Michael Schrage has pointed out, must fill a marketplace need. Media consumers do not want more of the same programming and are not going to pay $20 a month for something that is only marginally different from what they get "free."

This is why the cable efforts that stand to succeed tend to be counterprogramming ventures. James C. Crimmins's "Business Times" on the ESPN cable network offers hard business news opposite the early morning network shows. Crimmins got the idea out of frustration: He was traveling around the country and could get only what he calls "chit chat" on his hotel room TV while getting dressed. "Business Times" has a potential audience of 28 million homes on ESPN, which has brought in thirty-plus blue chip advertisers.

3. Newer is not always better.

It's no secret that some of the new entries into the media business are political conservatives from outside the news and information establishments. *USA Today* is the progeny of the old Gannett chain of Rochester, New York; Ted Turner is a self-proclaimed maverick and patriot who has announced his intention to knock over the established networks. The Australian Rupert Murdoch, the newest and brashest major media force, came to the United States a decade ago declaring a populist conservative creed. American publishers were out of touch, he said. "Papers and magazines in this country are written to please Madison Avenue and the friends of the publishers. They have lost touch with the desires of the reading public." Murdoch then proceeded to launch and/or buy a string of newspapers and magazines to advance his views: among them, the *National Star*, the *San Antonio Express*, the *New York Post*, *New York* magazine, *The Village Voice* weekly, the *Boston Herald*, and most recently, the *Chicago Sun-Times*.

When the news and information outputs of these new voices are measured, however, the results are somewhat dismaying, both to political conservatives and to adherents of journalistic excellence. Not public policy but entertainment proves to be their agenda.

Cable News Network runs business and financial coverage that is far superior to the offerings of the Big Three networks, according to a recent analysis by the Media Institute in Washington. But the Institute neglected to note the latest direction at CNN: Its extended coverage of the Big Dan's Tavern rape trial in New Bedford, Massachusetts, has been followed by a CNN decision to televise the Manhattan Beach, California, trial involving charges of sexual abuse of children at a preschool. A CNN executive told the *New York Times* that the Turner network doesn't want to "appear to be on a smut roll," but added that the decision to cover the trial was influenced by parents who said the problem of sexual abuse of children has been neglected. This "public interest" explanation is routinely offered by the established networks when they pursue the prurient.

Even Press Lord Murdoch, with his outspoken political agenda and record of playing kingmaker in Australia, has taken the low road of the 4Ss—sex, sports, sensation, and Studio 54—in his American properties much more often than the course of advocate of free enterprise. Harold Evans, in his new book *Good Times, Bad Times*, describes his many tangles with Murdoch when the Australian acquired *The Times* of London. Proud of a long *Times* enterprise piece about Solidarity and the depredations of the government's martial law crackdown, Evans showed the spread to Murdoch. The publisher said nothing. Later, Murdoch pointed to a two-paragraph story about Poland in one of his other properties, a scandal sheet: "That's all Poland should get," he explained. Interestingly, the one editorial property that Murdoch leaves alone is his *Village Voice*, which turns a small profit by appealing to its liberal-left, below-14th Street audience.

4. The centrist establishment still lives (it never went away).

If the new breed of media entrepreneurs has largely disappointed consumers—like the readers of this magazine —who had hoped for a fresh journalism rather than for more downscale entertainment, then their despair is not warranted. It's not as if they have no place to turn. Despite the image of a media dominated by liberals, the reality is much different. The most widely distributed syndicated columnists are conservatives James J. Kilpatrick (514 dailies) and George Will (375); centrists like Evans and Novak (143) and Joseph Kraft (137) and such straight-out liberals as Mary McGrory (160) and William Raspberry (150) trail badly. (This list excludes the two most popular syndicated columnists, Jack Anderson (675 dailies) and Art Buchwald (523), because neither is strictly a political commentator.

Elsewhere in print, the two biggest magazines are both conservative in their political outlook: *Readers' Digest* and *TV Guide*. So are the editorial pages of the two largest circulation papers in the country—the *Wall Street Journal* and the *New York Daily News*. Even in broadcasting, where liberal demons are said to infest the air, the conservative voice of Paul Harvey carries farther than any big-city, statist commentator. Also, despite all the charges about liberal bias in the network newscasts, the best serious studies of ABC, CBS, and NBC—by Michael Robinson at George Washington University, James David Barber and colleagues for the Social Science Research Council, and our own News Study Group at MIT—detected no ideological slanting of the news. What a number of us did find, however, was (again) much more provocative: a bias for the visual over the abstract, the anecdotal over the analytical and, above all, a preference for the steady standards of what I call

"olds" rather than news. These olds are stories about White House In Conflict With Congress (*any* White House, *any* Congress) and, from beyond the beltway, Heartland Twisters, California Life Styles, and Endangered Animals (in the trade, "Bambi's Mother stories").

News that's Fit to Print

The structural troubles with network news are beyond the scope of this article; they could fill a book—and they have: Robinson's, Barber's, mine. The audience, we've found at MIT, returns the compliment of superficial news: Viewers give it superficial attention.

Naturally, our leaders don't see it that way. They act as if they believe that what the establishment press says is important, that it is an agenda setter, that it tells people what to think *about*, if not what to think. This habit of fear is hard to break. Alexander Haig figured it all out in his new book. As he writes: "It is easy enough to remember, when one is greeting the voters in Indiana, that most Americans do not read the *New York Times* and the *Washington Post*, or watch the evening news on ABC, CBS, and NBC—or, for that matter, believe everything they read in newspapers and magazines or watch on television or hear on radio." But once the candidate gets to Washington, Haig goes on, "this memory tends to become submerged. . . ." The capital becomes the universe: "If I am so famous that the *Washington Post* is writing about me, then, of course, the whole world is reading it."

The whole world isn't reading or watching, at least not any one consistent line—that's the good news about the news. The bad news is that the range of opinion available is still too limited. After David Shaw of the *Los Angeles Times* interviewed some 100 people over a two-month period for his thorough-going article on political columnists, he concluded that the political dialogue in America, as conducted in newspapers, doesn't wander far from the establishment center.

There is hope. The *Wall Street Journal*'s editorial and op-ed pages, edited by Robert Bartley, are one of the few places where readers can find anything beyond the safe center; Bartley regularly runs liberals, conservatives, free enterprisers, libertarians, and even a genuine socialist, Alexander Cockburn. Among magazines, there are signs of alternatives to the great weekly blending machines of the middle. On the left, *Mother Jones* offers lively provocations while *The Nation* and *The New Republic* sparkle, proving there is nothing like having an incumbent administration to run against. For me, one of the pleasures of the National Magazine Awards at the Waldorf-Astoria in late April was the appearance of such finalists as *Texas Monthly*, *Ohio Magazine*, and *Third Coast* as exemplars of excellence in journalism. *Newsweek* and *U.S. News* were represented in the finals by their respective anniversary issues (Happy Birthday to Me!), while *High Technology*, based in Boston, was offering a superior analysis of the cruise missile, and *Outside* magazine—nice symbol, that—was winning an award for its general excellence in coverage of such stories as Western open spaces.

Finally, whatever growing pains cable and the new media are suffering, energy is clearly shifting in broadcasting. Thanks to CNN's twenty-four-hour news services, viewers need no longer wait until 7 p.m. for national news developments, or stay up until 11:30 for election results. The same open wire that brings sex-and-sensation courtroom drama into homes was also capable of bringing an eye-opening special like the Soviet Ministry of Defense's news conference from Moscow after the downing of KAL Flight 007. The existence of CNN has allowed the three networks to move their evening newscasts a little away from the traditional hot-off-the-wires approach.

Perhaps ten years from now, when the establishment and the upstarts, the insiders and the outsiders, the liberals and conservatives, are surveyed again, it will be possible to say of them what one great journalist, Lincoln Steffens, said of another great journalist, Jacob Riis, in another century: He not only got the news, he cared about the news.   ☑

Edwin Diamond *is an adjunct professor in the department of political science at the Massachusetts Institute of Technology, where he heads the News Study Group. His forthcoming book,* The Spot: The Rise of Political Advertising on Television, *will be published in June by the MIT Press.*

Selected AEI Publications